THE
GOLFER'S
ALPHABET

A CELEBRATION OF GOLF FROM A TO Z

by Kenneth G. Hess
photographs by Ron Coppock

THE
GOLFER'S
ALPHABET
A CELEBRATION OF GOLF FROM A TO Z

by Kenneth G. Hess
photographs by Ron Coppock

SIMON AND SCHUSTER

New York   London   Toronto   Sydney   Tokyo   Singapore

SIMON AND SCHUSTER

Simon & Schuster Building
Rockefeller Center
1230 Avenue of the Americas
New York, New York 10020

Designed by Kenneth G. Hess/SOMERSAULT BOOKS
Manufactured in the United States of America

1 3 5 7 9 10 8 6 4 2

Library of Congress Cataloging-in-Publication Data
Hess, Kenneth G.
The golfer's alphabet : a celebration of golf from A to Z / by Kenneth G. Hess ;
photographs by Ron Coppock.
p.   cm.
ISBN 0-671-74882-3 : $14.95
1. Golf—Collectibles.   2. Golf—Collectibles—Pictorial works.   3. Alphabet rhymes.
I. Title.
GV967.H52   1992   796.352'02—dc20   91-38342   CIP

To our wonderful wives,

Sudi and Linda

and to golf widows one and all.

AUTHOR'S NOTE

The following rhymes are meant to be read aloud, whether to yourself or, preferably, to a large rowdy group of golfers. Recite them in good health. Each of these magnificent photographs is both a tribute to the ancient game of golf and an illustration for your visual enjoyment. Savour them often.

a

A is for Addition.

And you'll find before you're through,

That as the round progresses,

It's all you seem to do.

B is for the Birdie,

A scarce "Bird", I'm afraid.

Seems everybody's heard of one,

Yet so few are ever made.

C

C is for the golf Club

That all golfers loathe to choose.

'Cuz no matter which you've chosen,

It's the Club that made you lose.

V W x Y z a ℬ 𝒞 D E f g H i J

D

D is for your Driver.

Not the one that Drives your car.

The one your ball is Driven with;

Sometimes straight and rarely far.

W x Y z a *B* **C D** E *f* *g* **H** i *J* k

E

E is for the Eagle,

That you made while out alone.

Too bad your luck was destined

To be forever unbeknown.

f

F is first in "Fore!"

'Cuz Fore's your only right

To yell and scream in anguish,

Warning those of your ball's flight.

Y z a *B* **C D** E *f* **g** H i *j* k **L m**

g

G is for those distant Greens.

To reach them is our goal.

Then, finally, once we get there,

Our new goal becomes the hole.

z a *B* **C D** E *f* **g** H i *J* k L **m** *n*

H

H is for the Hazards,

The Horrors of the game.

Those Hideous obstructions,

That should be this game's name.

i

I is for "I found it!"

The ball found in the rough.

It seems that every duffer's

Cried, "I found it!", quite enough.

J

J is for the Jackass.

For on the seventh tee,

The others in your foursome found

You shot "5", wrote "4", bragged "3".

k

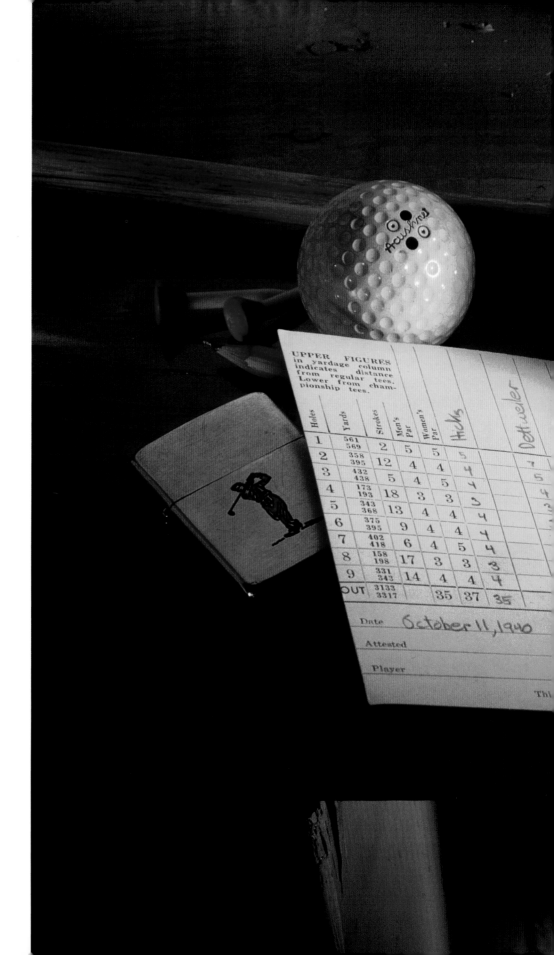

K is for the Kissing

Of your ball, your clubs, your tee;

'Cuz luck is either your best friend

Or your worst enemy.

D E f g H i ʃ k L m n O p Q R

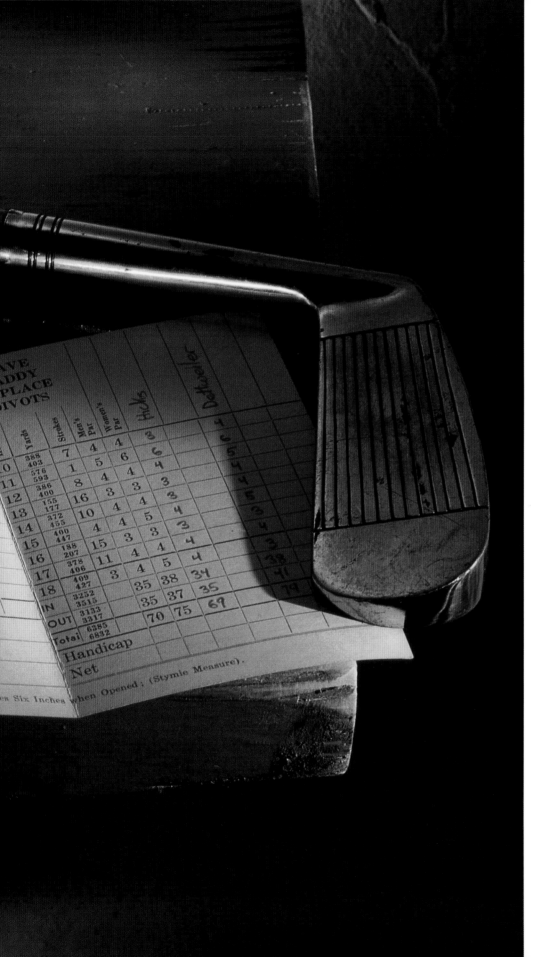

L

L is for the Links,

Your most favorite place to be.

Where duffers, drunks and amateurs

All meet to take some tee.

m

M is for the Mulligan

You'll take on number three.

The thing you didn't count on

Was you'd hit the only tree.

n

N is for old Niblicks.

Remember spoons and cleeks?

Your new excuse for slicing

Is you're playing with antiques.

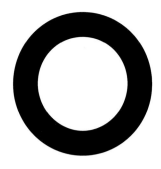

O is for your Old swing.

The pro called it a "hack".

There's a lesson in here somewhere

'Cuz you want your old hack back.

p

P is first in Par;

That standard, we adore it.

Too bad, that few will ever know

Precisely how to score it!

i J k L m n O p Q R s T u V W

Q is for the Quiet

Regulations do require.

So even when they shank it,

Hold your breath and just admire.

R is for the Read,

The way the green is layin'.

They say the most effective way

Is down low, as if you're prayin'.

S

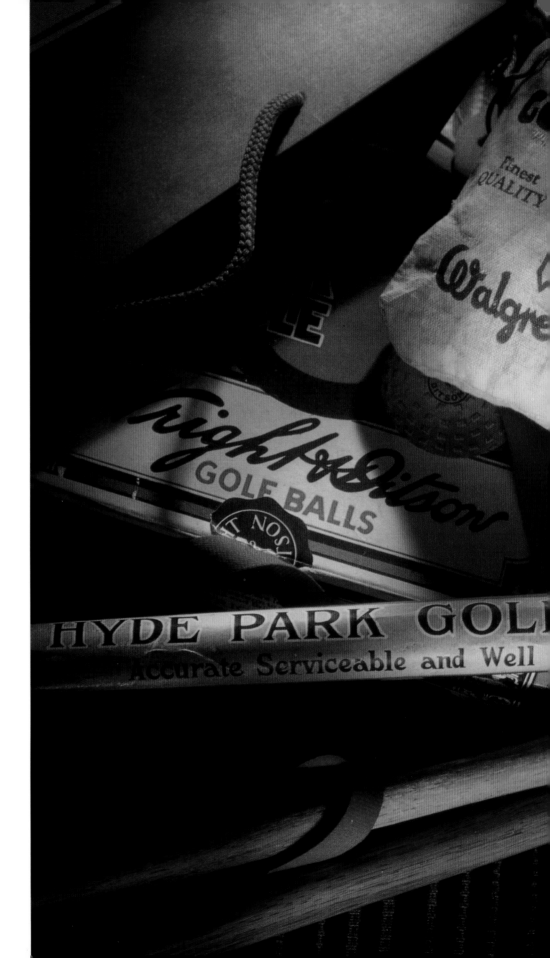

S is for the Sand

That seems misplaced without a beach.

Instead it's everywhere you look,

Making par so hard to reach.

T

T is for those little Tees

You're buying by the pound.

Trouble is, without them,

You can't get one off the ground.

m n O p Q R s T u V W x Y z a

U

U is the Umbrella

That you cart around in vain.

Leave it home, a downpour's certain.

Keep one close so it won't rain.

V

V is for that Voodoo.

It's what made that last shot fall.

It's not your swing that's faulty.

It's Voodoo on your ball.

W's for Water.

That is somehow magnetized.

Seems everytime we're near some,

Our game is compromised.

X is for that ugly X

You write when over ten.

But be sure to use a pencil.

You can't change it with a pen.

QRsTuVWxYZaBCDE

Y

Y is for those long, long Yards

And you've walked every one.

There's "nineteen" in the distance!

Now, it's time to have some fun.

R s T u V W x Y z a B C D E f

Z

Z just stands for Zero.

'Cuz we all know low beats high.

Therefore, the best score made in golf,

Can be made just sippin' rye.

s T u V W x Y z a B C D E f g

ACKNOWLEDGMENTS

The author and photographer would like to thank all of the people and organizations that helped make this book possible: Alan Kellock, Sylvia Angell, Bob Bows, Larry Lawrence, Gene Coppola, Bill Zmistowski, Jr., Mr. Elbert Hoppe of Chester Illinois, The Dooher Family of Vail: Nancy, Gerry, Nick, Elizabeth and Bilbo, Bal Patterson of The Page book store on the Mall in Boulder, George O'Belmito of Briar Place Pipes in Boulder, Somersault Books, Graphis Inc., Michael Weston, Patty Leasure, Joanne Barracca, Linda Cunningham, Stephen "Coz" Monseu, John Hickman, Tom Chenault (NuSkin), Don Meyers, George Raffensperger, Gilbert and Elanore Johnson, A.J. and especially Sudi, Linda, Nick, Towner, Tether, Axel and Gus. You're the best!

Now get out there and remember to keep your head down.

CREATIVE PENCIL DRAWING

CREATIVE

NEWBURGH FERRY TO BEACON

PENCIL DRAWING

Paul Hogarth

WATSON-GUPTILL PUBLICATIONS, INC.
New York

ACKNOWLEDGMENTS

I was greatly encouraged and helped in the writing of this book by my wife, Patricia, and it is to her that the book is affectionately dedicated.

Special thanks are also due to Donald Holden of Watson-Guptill, whose idea it was and whose tactful coaxing made me finish the book over a sustained and intensive period of traveling.

Special appreciation is also due to my friend, Ronald Searle, for his introduction.

I am no less indebted to the Hutchinson Publishing Group, London; Cassell and Company, London; Doubleday and Company, New York; Bernard Geis Associates, New York; The Macmillan Company, New York; Penguin Books, England; Oxford University Press, England; Lawrence and Wishart, London; Thomas Nelson and Sons, New York; The Limited Editions Club, New York; Denis Dobson, Ltd., London; Wydawnictwo Artystczno-Graficzne, Warsaw; the editors of *Fortune* and *Life;* the London *Sunday Times;* the ACA Gallery, New York; and the Shelbourne Hotel, Dublin, all of whom have allowed me to include drawings either in their possession or before publication.

For friendly assistance, valuable information, and loan of photographs, I should also like to thank Miss Estelle Mandel, my art agent in New York; Hope Leresche, my literary agent in the United Kingdom; Bernard Quint, art director of *Life;* Charles Rosner; Hans Schmoller of Penguin Books; Hugh Williamson of the Hutchinson Publishing Group; and certainly not least, Deirdre Amsden for her admirably concise illustrations for Chapter 2.

The owner's permission to reproduce works not in my possession, or works not in my publisher's possession, is gratefully acknowledged after each caption.

PAUL HOGARTH
East Bergholt, England
April, 1964

CONTENTS

THAT OTHER Hogarth—the great 18th Century English painter, William Hogarth—who was not exactly consistent in his thoughts, is on record in one of his sweeping moments, as saying that he was too keenly interested in human nature to interpose a sketchbook between himself and life. Besides, the power to represent what he saw with more or less accuracy came to him so easily, and with so little conscious learning, that he regarded drawing from nature as scarcely distinguishable from copying the work of other men.

Unfortunately, we are not all William Hogarths, and have not that rare ability to store in the mind most of what the eye selects. Happily, he did not entirely believe in following these dogmatic statements; nor did a thousand artists before and after him. The art collections of the world are richer and more fascinating for it.

Everyone has drawn and explored with a pencil or a crayon from the moment it was placed in his childish fist. A child draws before it writes, and so it has been since the Caveman doodled his first magical sign on the nearest rock with a charcoal ember.

There are few draftsmen today so well qualified to speak authoritatively "from the field" as it were, than Paul Hogarth. Battle-scarred and articulate, experienced and dedicated, he earned his knowledge and mastery of the medium the hard, probing way.

Paul Hogarth and I have known each other a long time. Soon after the war, we made a couple of journeys together, working side by side in shattered cities among hungry people. We often shared the same models in the street, usually under the inevitable crush of a shaggy Balkan crowd. We gathered a lot of material on these trips, quite a few fleas, and what is more important, a little more understanding of human nature.

The lines on a face say something to everyone. But the attitude of the man caught on the hop, going about his business; the anxiety to want to be a good model; the self-important stance to be put on record before a grinning, bantering press of public nuisances—all these tell one a great deal more than the subject bargained for. The simple sketch turns swiftly before your eyes into a personal comment and the moment is uniquely pinned down.

William Hogarth did not mean that drawing from nature was tantamount to plagiarism of the most boring kind. He meant, in his badly expressed way, that slavish recording was a waste of time. The eye may select, but the brain must revaluate. A drawing does not dribble through the eye, down through the fingers, and out onto the paper. Thought and a point-of-view make the artist. A technician is merely a technician.

But, thank heaven, there is great pleasure in drawing, and that is what Paul Hogarth communicates. He is the artist who is also the enthusiast. He takes his work seriously, but he does not let it rule him. And he enjoys himself, which after all is one of the prime reasons for wanting to draw at all.

Rules are there to be broken; materials are there to be experimented with and dominated; ideas are everywhere to be snatched from the air and pinned onto paper.

Whatever you do, wherever you go, there will always be something to draw. You only need three things: a pencil, a notebook, and your head.

Who better than Paul Hogarth to tell you how best to use them. As Shakespeare says: Go to!

RONALD SEARLE
Paris, 1964

Art begins when a man wishes to immortalize the most vivid moment he has ever lived.

ARTHUR SYMONS

1 THE ART OF PENCIL DRAWING

IF ANYONE asked me why I became a draftsman, I might answer as most artists would: I do not really know, except that I always wanted to be one. If pressed, I might add that I could not work as painters do, completely alone. I was restless in my studio and wanted an audience to which I could project. I wanted to get out into the world and draw. I had what Gauguin called the "terrible itch for the unknown."

But if you asked me how I equipped myself to be a draftsman, I think there is a simple answer: I equipped myself chiefly by moving around and seeing as much of the world as I possibly could. In doing so, I learned to draw the world at large.

Learning by experience

At art school, however, I soon discovered that the techniques I needed were not taught. Art teachers can pass judgment only on what they themselves know. This knowledge is usually limited in scope, as too few teachers are practicing artists. So I set myself the task of becoming a draftsman by first hand experience.

The pursuit of experience was also a search for self. And this can take an artist in many directions. For many years I felt myself to be little more than a committed observer, called upon to set down the scene before me. Only in recent years have I also reproduced the feelings the scene might arouse. And as the years go by, the more vulnerable I become: my feelings are intensified.

Ben Shahn defines art as arising from something stronger than stimulation or even inspiration. It may, he said, take fire from something closer to provocation, being *compelled* by life.

Developing a personal vision

I would add that we have to express ourselves in order to assert our personalities, to establish a relationship with ourselves. We can then turn to life to record our impressions; to interpret our feelings; to establish intellectual concepts. My own struggles to externalize various hopes and fears, frustrations and admirations, can be found in drawings throughout this book.

For many reasons, therefore, it could be said that the majority of artists are merely men and women searching to evolve a means of *understanding*.

I have found pencil drawing especially suitable for the development of my own understanding, just as others gain understanding by painting or making movies. A wide range of personal style and technique can be based on the vast variety of combinations of charcoal, wax, and graphite, both in black and color. This variety gives the pencil a remarkable flexibility and ease as a graphic medium.

This book deals mainly with how I feel about drawing and how my personal vision is formed. Although there are no rules to this game, I hope this book will help you to build your own mastery of all the pencil media, your own artistic vision, as well as your pleasure in drawing.

14

MANHATTAN PEANUTS

IN SLATTERY'S BAR, DUBLIN, 1959 The spontaneity
of pencil media is shown here in this rapidly-made
drawing. Drawn with a stick of natural willow charcoal
on Abbey Mill paper. From *Brendan Behan's Island,*
1962. Courtesy, Hutchinson Publishing Group, London,
and Bernard Geis Associates, New York.

ARMENIAN PEASANTS, USSR, 1957   This drawing was made on a visit to
Russia in 1957. The English painter, Derrick Greaves, and I had flown
down to Erivan from Moscow for a few days. One day, tiring of interpre-
ters and conducted tours, we cut loose and roamed around the countryside.
I drew this scarred, noble countenance in a field of giant sunflowers against
Mount Ararat. It was one of those occasions when you see a face and feel
you must draw it. The extraordinary thing was that my wishes were understood and the peasant sat for me for a good hour. I sought to express his
character with maximum sympathy, as the man had such dignity and
strength. Drawn on Italian Fabriano paper with a soft Hardtmuth charcoal
lead. Soft charcoal lead is ideal for portraits in which you need strength
of interpretation.

THE EXECUTION OF ESSEX   One of a series of historical magazine illustrations made early in 1964. The stronger the illustration, the more the interest of the reader is focused on the subject or the story. The problem here was to recreate the atmosphere or the events of the past in such a way that they might be readily understood. Drawn with Caran d'Ache charcoal lead, 4B and 6B Eagle Charco pencils, and 6B Venus graphite pencil, augmented with passages of Winsor & Newton gouache color on Hollingworth Kent Mill paper. From the special Shakespeare number of *Life*, April 23, 1964. Courtesy *Life* Magazine © Time, Inc.

DUTCH REFORMED CHURCH, HYDE PARK, NEW YORK, 1963 When I use color with pencil media, I first wash on the color, then draw when the surface is thoroughly dry. This time, I tried it the other way round, because I was working against the failing daylight. This worked out because the strip effect of lateral wooden planking was what I wanted; therefore, I did not need to draw with pencil on top of the wash. Pelikan watercolors were used, plus 4B and 6B Venus graphite pencils. Saunders paper.

THE STATE CAPITOL, ALBANY, NEW YORK, 1963   Graphite pencil and
watercolor is an ideal combination for this type of drawing. The intricate
splendor of the mid-nineteenth century civic style can be well expressed
by a loose, yet stylized drawing. I used 5B and 6B Venus graphite pencils,
augmented with passages of Pelikan watercolor and Higgins manuscript
ink. Saunders paper.

PARACHUTE RIDE, CONEY ISLAND, NEW YORK, 1963   Close observation
of both character and movement is possible with the graphite lead pencil.
Drawn in a 14 x 17 Rich Art sketchbook with 5B and 6B Venus graphite
pencils. From *Brendan Behan's New York,* 1964. Courtesy, Hutchinson
Publishing Group, London, and Bernard Geis Associates, New York.

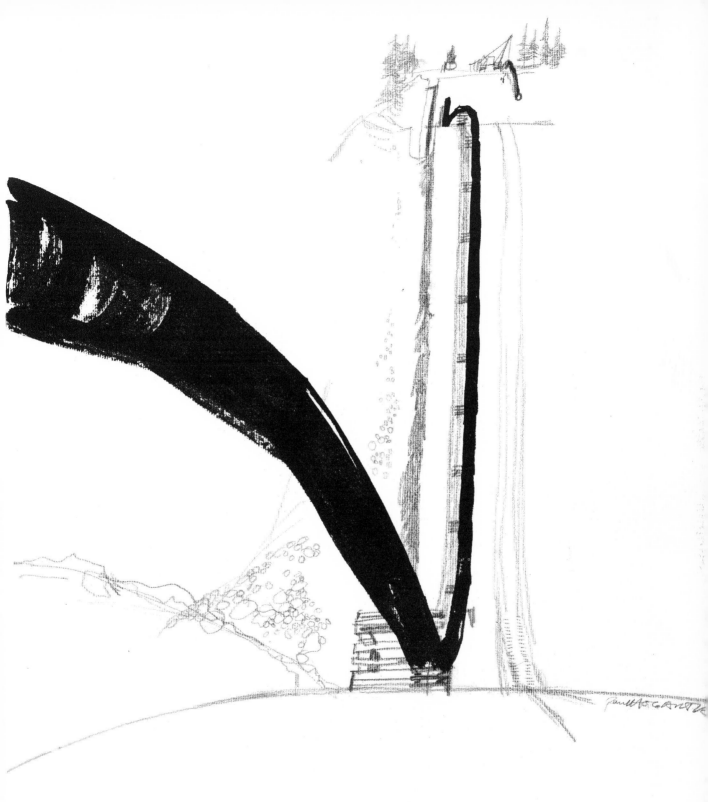

PIPELINE IN ALABAMA, 1962   Reportorial drawing for *Fortune*. Bent to
fit the rolling hills of Alabama, the pipeline is ready to be lowered into
the ditch. To emphasize the fact, I used a black ink brush line and re-
stricted my pencil work to supporting detail. Higgins manuscript ink and
4B Eagle Charco pencil on Strathmore charcoal paper. Courtesy, *Fortune*
Magazine © February, 1963, Time, Inc.

21

DRAWING FOR *Little Men*
A drawing in charcoal pencil and ink wash for a book illustration, by its very nature, turns the attention of the reader to a specific incident, creating a mood which greatly enhances the appeal of certain books. Drawn with 4B and 6B Eagle Charco pencils, with passages of rubbed Chinese stick ink, on Saunders paper. From *Little Men* by Louisa May Alcott. Courtesy, The Macmillan Company, New York, 1963.

2 MATERIALS AND TOOLS FOR DRAWING

Most artists use materials without conscious thought. They do not deliberately select a particular degree of graphite or charcoal pencil to draw with. In their haste to catch an idea on the wing, they seize whatever pencil might be near at hand. Any pencil could well be the best choice. This element of uncertainty encourages improvisation and lends spontaneity and vitality.

Although you must be aware of materials and their exact use, you should not allow yourself to be *dominated* by them. Do not make a fetish of buying everything offered in your local art materials store. Your materials and tools are but a means to an end.

A sensitive awareness of everyday imagery—the pictorial content of the world around you—is of far greater importance.

Nevertheless, an artist must have confidence in his equipment. This is especially necessary if you are making one drawing after another, for several days or even weeks. When you make this kind of sustained, continuous effort—when you want every drawing to be successful—then you need to rely on your materials for consistent performance. They should be carefully chosen.

Begin with simple equipment

Today, the range and variety of tools, materials, and equipment are immense. In principle, you should try all that might be applied to drawing. But at first your tools should be few, so you can more easily master their use.

For a long time, I used nothing but two charcoal pencils—soft and hard—razor blades, and a bottle of fixative, all carried around in a tobacco pouch. I made many elaborate drawings with these simple materials. For when you use nothing but one or two degrees of a given pencil, you are more inclined to push the tool's potentialities to the very maximum.

You can then go ahead and use more degrees, as well as color, pen line, wash, and other techniques which combine effectively with pencil.

Pencils, crayons, and other tools

When I speak of pencil drawing, I mean not only the common graphite pencil, but the scores of leads, chalks, and crayons that fit between your fingers or in a mechanical holder.

HOLDERS Unlike sticks of natural charcoal, leads of refined charcoal rarely break if used in push-action holders, which are available in a wide range of designs to hold leads of various sizes and shapes. These in particular are the ones I like drawing with: *(1) Hardtmuth* 5644B. This is an early type, suitable for rapid work. The smooth, round stem is perhaps a disadvantage. This holder will take all medium size leads (of all degrees) up to 3″ long. *(2) Caran d'Ache* 12. The durable hexagonal stem inspires maximum confidence. Suitable for heavily accented drawings of large size, this will take all leads of the thickest diameter, up to 4″ in length. *(3) Conté* 580. I first discovered this in 1952 and used it for many years. At that time it was not widely used by artists and was difficult to obtain outside France. It is designed for the Pierre Noir leads of all degrees. These leads are usually 6″ long. *(4) Koh-i-Noor Super-versatil* 827. Thinner than the Conté 580, this has the feel of a pencil. It is designed for Hardtmuth leads of all degrees, up to 6″ in length. *(5) Caran d'Ache Fixpencil.* This is one of the latest designs. The portion held by the fingers is roughened to ensure non-slip grip, which is useful as fingers do perspire freely at times. It will take leads of all degrees up to approximately 4½″ long.

1   2   3   4   5

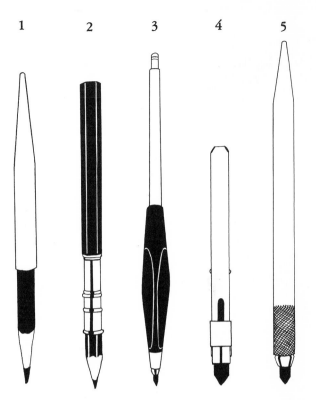

HOLDERS Graphite sticks or leads handle more easily in holders. I also use holders to extend the length of graphite pencils. *(1) Grifhold 64.* The pencil screws inside this aluminum pencil lengthener. *(2) Rowney 1018 Pencil Lengthener.* This sleeve type is for round or hexagonal pencils. The sliding ring tightens and holds the pencil. Also made by Faber, Hardtmuth, and Winsor & Newton. *(3) Faber-Castell Tekagraph.* This well designed German push-action holder is for graphite leads. It has an excellent grip and is suitable for precise, detailed work. This model will take all degrees up to 6″ in length. *(4) Square Pastel Holder.* This is suitable for square-shaped graphite sticks and especially for colored charcoal sticks or pastels. Made by Faber and Hardtmuth. *(5) Grifhold 134.* This aluminum lead holder has a milled grip. A well balanced, useful holder, it will take all medium and large diameter leads.

These tools come in great variety, but my own drawing media fall into three categories: charcoal and the various chalks, crayons, and carbon leads that handle like charcoal; graphite; and oil-bound chalks or crayons.

Charcoal leads, charcoal pencils, carbon pencils, Conté and Hardtmuth crayons and leads, are the modern equivalent of the traditional charcoal stick. They are easier and more reliable for use outside the studio. The traditional stick of natural charcoal tends to break unexpectedly under the strain of rapid drawing; it is really suitable only for use indoors, as great care is needed to handle and preserve such drawings. Although they are strengthened by refining and processing, the newer leads are almost as fragile; but they rarely break if used in push-action plastic or metal holders.

A wider variety of line is possible with these leads, as they are made in different weights and thicknesses. Great flexibility of hand movement is possible if you use them in a holder, rather than in pencil form. The holder should be hexagonal in shape: this allows a firmer, easier, non-slip grip. Leads in a holder are generally more suitable for large drawings with plenty of dramatic emphasis and tonal density. Charcoal pencils, on the other hand, are usually better for tighter drawings of a more purely linear nature. Compared to charcoal pencils—which do wear down to the wood very quickly—I find that charcoal leads in holders stand up better to the faster pace of drawing on a large scale.

Conté and Hardtmuth—in my opinion—reign supreme as the best makers of leads for use in holders. I especially recommend Conté's Pierre Noir Mines, leads which are very slightly larger than the thickness of an ordinary pencil and are graded from 1 to 6. Hardtmuth leads, however, are best when thick and soft. These are graded in extra soft, soft, medium, and hard.

Leads are also available in color, square in shape and boxed like pastels. Swan's Othello series I find to be excellent.

Charcoal pencils are usually made in four degrees: hard, medium, soft, and extra soft. I prefer to work with Conté and Hardtmuth; but when I have used Eagle's Charco pencils I have found these to be just as good. Blaisdell charcoal pencils are also recommended; these are wrapped in a paper cylinder, with a pull-thread for self-sharpening.

Common graphite pencils are more suitable for stylized or precise drawing, particularly when greater definition of detail is required. These pencils are available in a great variety of hardness and softness; I find 2B, 3B, 5B, and 6B most useful. Venus, Royal Sovereign, and Faber I have found to be best for my purposes.

Graphite is also available in round, rectangular, and square shaped sticks for use in a holder. These are usually made in degrees of 2B, 4B, and 6B. There are also oval shaped graphite pencils originally made for the use of carpenters. These are larger to hold and have big, flat leads which usually come in three degrees: 2B, 4B, and 6B. The sticks and pencils are both useful for rapid, broad work.

Finally, there are the oil-bound chalks or crayons which are especially suitable for work on high quality papers. These chalks are available in colors, as well as in black. The most reliable of this type are those made by Conté and Hardtmuth. Drawings made with these crayons do not usually require fixing. The oily or waxy content of these chalks will prevent your drawings from smudging.

Papers

The right paper is vital to the success of a drawing, particularly if you work on location. I usually work on loose sheets of paper rather than on a pad or sketchbook. I carry a varied selection of colors and textures suitable for different kinds of drawings. The loose sheets are clipped to a light weight piece of hardboard.

Choice of a paper is largely conditioned by whether you are drawing for yourself, for reproduction, or for both. If for yourself, choose any paper suitable for charcoal or graphite pencils. This should be any good quality white cartridge, heavy bond, or similar drawing paper, either smooth or slightly surfaced.

If you are drawing for reproduction, your choice of paper depends on what process will be used to reproduce your drawing. Your actual drawing *technique* will determine effective and exact reproduction; but the right choice of paper will help you relax and forget any inhibitions about direct drawing for reproduction.

A good *laid* paper has a surface of fine parallel lines, which ensure that the pencil strokes are sufficiently broken up to make your drawing more easily reproduced by the line process.

The techniques of drawing for reproduction are discussed more fully in Chapter 3.

Machine made, cotton fiber, *laid* paper has the quality of hand made paper. Its slightly ribbed surface offers a sympathetic texture for all types of pencil drawing. There are several excellent kinds: the French, Italian, and American papers of the Ingres type (which generally have a more emphatic surface); the more subtle English Saunders paper; and Strathmore charcoal paper in the United States. Both Strathmore and Ingres charcoal papers are available in colors and can also be obtained in the form of sketchbooks.

A smooth (hot pressed) white paper is also ideal for most kinds of pencil drawing. Strathmore and Hollingworth Kent Mill are highly recommended.

Hand made papers, however, still offer the most perfect surface for pencil drawing, and I must admit to a consuming weakness for them. I stock up whenever the opportunity presents itself on my travels. Smooth Whatman (no longer made, unfortunately) is a superb paper, but there are American, Dutch, French, and Italian equivalents, just as good as this classic paper. One of the finest surfaces I have ever drawn on was a Chinese paper, hand made from bamboo. This is manufactured in thin sheets, laminated to make up the weight you require, then color dyed to taste. It comes in great sheets, as uneven as bear skins, with a soft grain exquisitely suitable for pencil and wash.

Sketchbooks

If you prefer working in a sketchbook, you will find that many of the papers I have mentioned are available or can be made up in sketchbook form. Although having your chosen paper made up can be difficult and expensive in the United States and England, it is still fairly common practice in France, Italy, and Spain, where small binding workshops abound.

Sketchbooks are convenient under difficult working conditions. I also use them as notebooks. An 11 x 14 spiral bound book is useful for making complete drawings or studies on beaches, in bars, or other public places

STOOLS A good stool is indispensable for drawing outdoors. Although preferences vary, I find types 1, 2, and 3 too low for comfortable posture. A good one is well worth the extra cost. Here are five types I use at various times:

1

2

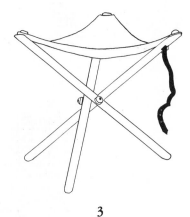

3

where additional equipment might attract undue attention. A smaller, pocket size sketchbook is handy for working in theaters and courts; for roughing out compositions; or for making notes of figures and details to be added later to a completed larger drawing. My own notes are usually little more than shorthand; I like sketchbooks of transparent paper because I can then develop a scribbled note by a combination of redrawing and tracing.

Fixatives

Fixative is a light spray of invisible lacquer which will ensure the permanence of your completed drawings, keeping them smudge-free in a drawer or portfolio. For charcoal and crayon drawings, you will need a heavy fixative; for carbon and graphite drawings, a lighter one will suffice.

Drawings are fixed by spraying the fixative at a slight angle with a mouth blower or a spray can. A spray can is best because a blower invariably gums up, and has to be cleaned out and readjusted. If you prefer a mouth blower, it is a good idea to have several blowers with you. Even then, they will not always work. I have carried as many as a dozen spares in my bag, but it can happen that none of the spares will function properly when you most need them.

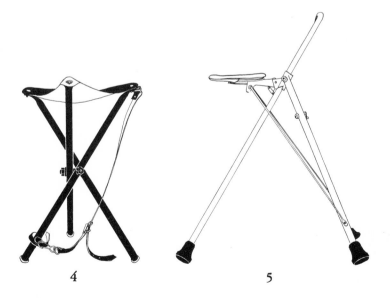

(1) Aluminum folding stool with canvas seat. This popular type is available in an emergency from most hardware stores and from Woolworth's *(2) Light folding wooden stool.* I have always found this one useful when drawing in cities. *(3) Russian fisherman stool.* This wooden model is comfortable but the canvas seat did not last. *(4) French tubular metal artist's stool, with leather seat and shoulder carrying strap.* The French make the best folding stools. I have lost at least three. *(5) English Hill-rest metal shooting stool.* This is light, very comfortable, and folds flat.

4   5

If you run out of ready-made fixatives in the middle of nowhere, you can make your own by mixing one part of shellac flakes or gum arabic balls to four parts of synthetic or pure alcohol.

Erasers

In an eraser, quality is most important. A good eraser efficiently eliminates unwanted lines and it will clean surfaces. A cheap one will not; or worse, it may deface your drawing.

There are many good ones to be recommended for general use. An eraser should be soft and pliable. I use three types. A gum eraser (so-called art gum), is soft and pliable and therefore does not mark or scratch the paper. The plastic or kneaded type I find excellent for soft graphite, pastel, and charcoal erasing. This is easily shaped with the fingers for cleaning fine detail. The Blaisdell paper-covered eraser is also useful as it is pencil-shaped, making it easier to erase detail without smudging. I also use the Faber Rub Kleen soft pencil eraser.

General equipment

In addition to pencils, you will need a pocket knife or blade (X-acto Number 100 is a good one), and half-a-dozen Esterbrook spring clips. I also recommend a lightweight collapsible stool. Pencils and erasers should be carried in separate containers or plastic bags to keep them clean. And everything should be carried in a roomy satchel (artist's or fisherman's type) in zippered plastic bags, so that liquids (such as fixatives and inks) can be isolated against internal disaster. A further precaution is to have your ink or fixative (if you do not use a spray can) in plastic bottles.

Finally, you should have a canvas, plastic, or zippered leather carrying case or portfolio in which to keep a sheet of hardboard, sketchbooks, and drawings dry and clean. This completes your equipment for working outdoors.

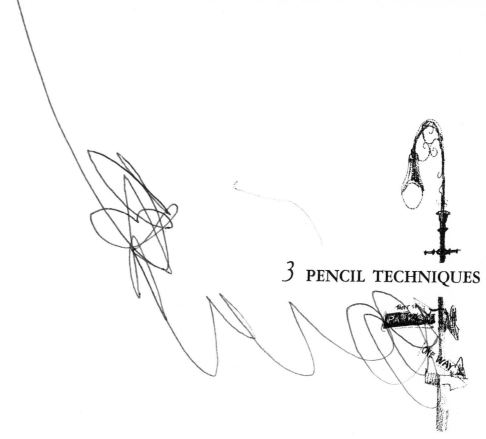

3 PENCIL TECHNIQUES

Pᴇɴᴄɪʟ ᴅʀᴀᴡɪɴɢ should be just as natural as the act of writing. I am not one of those who see drawing as a means of reconstructing nature, but as a means of interpreting a personal reaction to every kind of phenomenon, natural and man-made. We interpret our subconscious by doodling while telephoning or waiting, continuing the effortless imagery of childhood. This is the kind of relaxed fluency to strive for in drawing.

Any revival of the submerged pictorial vision of childhood must be based, of course, on an adult awareness of what you can actually do with your pencil media.

Learning pencil techniques

A good way to begin—although it is certainly not the only way—is to get used to drawing with only one or two degrees of charcoal or graphite lead. My personal preference is charcoal. I started with charcoal in rebellion against a life-class instructor's stupid insistence that *only* graphite pencils were to be used for drawing the model. Formal academic drawing is far from easy with the graphite pencil as it requires great coordination of hand and eye. Many years went by before I was really able to draw with the graphite pencil; in fact, I have only recently started using it again. Charcoal leads enabled me to forget those tortuous life classes, and enabled me to draw freely.

Start with whatever tool lets you feel at ease; but get thoroughly used to working with a medium or soft lead, so that you will be completely familiar with the idiosyncrasies of charcoal or graphite. Build up your drawing gradually by the use of line and texture. Spray lightly and frequently with fixative.

When you feel that this one lead restricts you, move on to two or three additional degrees *before* you widen your range still further and start using pen line or washes of ink and color. I myself moved slowly from one drawing medium to another, as though to undo the effects of bad training. With each step, I found that my confidence as a draftsman gradually increased.

But there is no reason why everyone should undergo this slow progression from one medium to another. Since the days when I was an art student, more practicing creative artists are teaching in art schools, both in Europe and in the United States. Chances are that if you are an art student, you are already used to working with a wide range of pencil media.

Improvised drawings

My various methods of working on location are fully described in the following chapters. But generally, when I work on location, I can decide only in the vaguest way on textural effects or tonal emphasis. Whether I draw with one degree of charcoal or graphite lead, with several degrees, or with mixed media, depends on the ideas I may get while I work.

COURT PERFORMANCE OF *Romeo and Juliet* BEFORE QUEEN ELIZABETH IN THE GREAT HALL OF GREENWICH PALACE A magazine illustration in graphite pencil, Caran d'Ache charcoal lead, and soft Hardtmuth charcoal lead, augmented with passages of gouache color and washes of diluted drawing ink. Originally reproduced in *Life* by letterpress in color. From the special Shakespeare number of *Life,* April 23, 1964. Courtesy, *Life* Magazine, © Time, Inc.

33

For instance, I might be drawing an elaborate facade with a 5B graphite pencil; I suddenly feel that the drawing will work only if a group of large heads, drawn emphatically in soft charcoal, move against the building. By shuffling or expanding my focus, I gamble partial success for total success, against the risk of total failure. When working on location, I like to feel that I can surprise myself.

Planned drawings

If my drawing is for a book or magazine, however, it is a completely different problem. Both these kinds of drawing do involve more conscious planning—more conscious realization of mood or period—right from the beginning.

After making the roughest visuals from a preliminary reading of a text, I move on to completely realized roughs, usually drawn in medium charcoal or soft graphite on tracing paper, the same size as the finished art will be.

I work in this way not only for the approval of an art editor or art director—roughs are sometimes requested to save any misunderstandings—but mainly to settle problems well in advance. I can then place the rough on a light table (a glass-topped table with built-in lights for tracing) and go ahead with a free interpretation and development on drawing paper. In my studio work, I continually incorporate anything new I may discover while working *outside* the studio. The illustrations I contribute to books and magazines really derive their strength from my location work.

Drawing for reproduction

Whether your purpose is reportorial, literary or editorial illustration, pencil media will give you a wide and flexible range of expression. If you look at the illustrations in this chapter alone, you will see the variety of dramatic effects that can be achieved with combinations of charcoal and graphite, with or without ink wash or color.

If your drawing is not for reproduction, all you have to consider is

NEW YORK STREET CORNER The fidelity of offset
makes it the best process for reproducing pencil drawings of every kind. The respective qualities of charcoal
lead and blotted penwork would be less faithfully reproduced by letterpress or gravure. From *Brendan Behan's
New York*, 1964. Courtesy, Hutchinson Publishing
Group, London, and Bernard Geis Associates, New York.

what pencil medium seems most appropriate for your chosen subject. Once this is settled, you can move ahead and let yourself go.

If you are working for reproduction, it is essential to consider the general limitations of the printing process that will be used to reproduce your drawing. Today, these limitations are relatively slight, compared to what they once were. There are few drawings in any medium that cannot be satisfactorily reproduced by at least one reproduction technique.

The point, of course, is that an assignment may specifically ask for drawings to be suitable for reproduction in a given process. This is why it is useful to be aware of the various limitations of each process. These limitations involve such minor modifications in drawing technique that I certainly do not feel them to be inhibiting.

Line reproduction

Let me take an example. If I am asked by a publisher or a newspaper to make a drawing for the line process—just black lines, no grays—then my drawing will have to be crisp black and white. This means I will have to make stronger, more heavily accented strokes and lines than may be usual. Textures or tonal effects will have to be rendered in a more stylized and linear technique. I can work with any degree of charcoal or graphite, except maybe the hardest; *but* I take care to make my drawing on a white, grained (laid) paper which breaks up the pencil strokes and lines sufficiently to make the drawing reproducible by the line process. The character of a pencil drawing, even when reproduced in black line, is thus very largely retained. This would not be the case if I used a smooth paper.

But sometimes I have not succeeded in turning out drawings which could be reproduced! In the *studio,* one works more deliberately and I can always see to it that my finished artwork is suitable for reproduction. In the heat of drawing on *location,* however, I may have overlooked the fact that elements of my drawing trail off into light gray lines and will not reproduce. Rather than lose any spontaneity by redrawing, I have sometimes had a high contrast photograph or photostat made. This darkens the lines of the drawing, while retaining its quality, and a good line plate can be made.

Halftone reproduction

Sometimes, in a mistaken effort to conserve the grays and delicate lines of a drawing, an art editor of a newspaper will have a halftone plate made. This process involves a screen of fine dots, which vary in density according to the quality of paper used. A newspaper halftone—with its very coarse screen of dots—generally reduces the impact of a drawing to the point of emasculation.

In magazines, however, the screen is much finer and the paper of better quality. In the glossier magazines printed by letterpress, the halftone screen can reproduce drawings most effectively.

If I am told that the process to be used is offset or photogravure, then I have little to worry about. I can work as if my drawings were not for reproduction at all. Delicate veils of tone will be preserved in the plate. Provided that my drawings are not *excessively* light or too large—reduction should not be more than 50%—any drawing can be faithfully reproduced by these processes.

CHAPTER HEADPIECE From an illustrated edition of *The Story of an African Farm* by Olive Schreiner (The Limited Editions Club, New York, 1962). The plates for the book were made by the Dow-Etch process, which faithfully retains the respective qualities of charcoal lead and pen line. Courtesy, The George Macy Companies, Inc.

DRAWINGS FOR *Little Men* These drawings were made for reproduction by the offset process, so I could freely use concentrated or diluted washes of drawing ink, combined with light and heavy accents in graphite and charcoal. I kept the drawings contrasty to ensure that reproduction would not only be sharp, but that they would look strong on the actual printed page. Both were drawn with 4B and 6B Eagle Charco pencils and diluted, rubbed Chinese stick ink. From *Little Men* by Louisa May Alcott. Courtesy, The Macmillan Company, New York, 1963.

BOOK JACKET   This book jacket drawing shows use of Conté charcoal lead, ink brush work, pen line combined with Zipatone. Reproduced in line. Courtesy, Oxford University Press, England, 1962.

J. M. SYNGE
FOUR PLAYS
AND
THE ARAN ISLANDS

ANOTHER BOOK JACKET This poster-type design was drawn twice the reproduction size in soft Hardtmuth charcoal lead on Ingres paper. Note the dispersed quality of the strokes, which enabled an excellent line plate to be made. The scarf was drawn in diluted drawing ink with a brush. Courtesy, Penguin Books, 1962.

ILLUSTRATION FROM AN EDITION OF THE *Short Stories of O. Henry*
This drawing was made with Conté Pierre Noir charcoal leads on Ingres
paper for reproduction by the line process (black and white, no grays).
Courtesy, The Folio Society, London, 1960.

4 DRAWING LANDSCAPE

Making complete drawings outdoors, rather than making outdoor *studies* for completion indoors, is an informal and stimulating method of working, for which the pencil media are especially suitable. Landscape drawing, in particular, is a good way to start.

The bustle and pressure of the city are much too distracting until you are used to working on location. In the city, I can seldom work for more than two hours at a time; in the country, I may spend the whole day patiently making several drawings of the same subject.

In the quiet of an orchard, a river bank, or the seashore, I welcome the lack of tension and noise. I am on my own, with enough peace and quiet to deepen my whole grasp of drawing; I can relax and be moved by the innate lyrical qualities in nature. Landscape drawing is a process of discovery; I seek to intensify the eternal, rather than observe the ephemeral.

The creative process

Sometimes the process is set off by various associations, compounded of images recalled from paintings or movies. Quite suddenly, I may be confronted with a scene in which a herd of hogs is led by a Circe-like girl along the stone-walled lane of a ripening Mediterranean orchard. The scene invokes the heady atmosphere of a Victorian academy painting of classical myths, plus the ominous undertones of a Bergman movie. The atmosphere completely possesses me; I know I must set it down on paper.

Although mood and atmosphere are primary factors which move me to draw landscape in any country, I often forget these qualities when I begin to draw. What emerges is an image in its own right, owing more to the inherent character of my natural surroundings—the structure and detail of the landscape—than to the transient associations of my subconscious mind.

Planning a drawing

Deciding *what* to draw and *how* can be as important as actually drawing. The more time I can spend roaming around, the better. I drive or walk around, absorbing impressions, making rough notes. These are immediate, spontaneous reactions which might be developed later into finished drawings when I return to the same spot. My notes are stimulated by elements which have textural or dramatic potentialities: trees against clear or clouded skies; crops or grass against stone; growth against decay; life against death. I scribble a "must" or "very good" or just plain "good" and I record the best time of day to return and draw it.

PAGE FROM MY MALLORCA NOTEBOOK (*Left*) This compositional note is for the drawing, "La Calobra." My notes read: "Rocks—Road to La Calobra. VG—a must! Extraordinary volcanic formations. Late afternoon light best."

LA CALOBRA, MALLORCA, 1963 (*Right*) The unquiet calm of a lunar-like landscape contrasts with the incised complexity of the rock formations. I used Blaisdell Speed-D-Point charcoal pencils—soft, medium, and hard—to convey the variety of linear emphasis. A 3B Faber graphite pencil was used for the more detailed drawing of the trees and grasses in the middle distance. From a forthcoming book on Mallorca with Robert Graves. Courtesy, Cassell and Company, London, and Doubleday and Company, New York.

In the summer, the best time would be either in the early morning, shortly after sunrise; or late afternoon; or perhaps early evening. I avoid the intense sunlight of mid-day, which tends to flatten the forms of incidental detail. Late afternoon light gives greater clarity and definition of detail. Towards evening, as the sun goes down and the shadows slowly lengthen, I know my subject will be charged with an atmosphere entirely absent during most of the day.

A Polaroid Land Camera or any other camera may be useful as a time-saver, especially for illustrators. Other than for an occasional illustration, I do not use a camera or photographic reference material. I have no rooted objection to the mechanical image produced by the camera; I find that relying on photographic material simply interferes with my personal sense of discovery.

Seize your subject while you can

But often I stumble across something I must draw there and then. This urge dates back to several drawing trips to China and eastern Europe in the fifties. Because I always traveled with an interpreter or guide and worked to a scheduled itinerary, I lived in a permanent state of subdued excitement; I wondered whether I would have time to get my drawings done at all; and having done them, I wondered whether they would come up to my own expectations. Passing through the breathtakingly spectacular landscape of South China in 1954, I saw scenes I would probably never ever see again. I had no choice but to make direct drawings at high speed in a mood of partially controlled frenzy!

This habit has remained so strong that whenever I feel I *must* stop to make a drawing, I find it difficult to persuade myself that I will be around for several weeks. I must force myself to be patient, look for my material, make notes, and return to make a final drawing. But I still give in to the habit of drawing on impulse, because being excited about my subject is *vital* to the success of my drawings. Moreover, I have to feel that there is an element of risk involved, that I really have to rise to the occasion, to capture something of its significance for me.

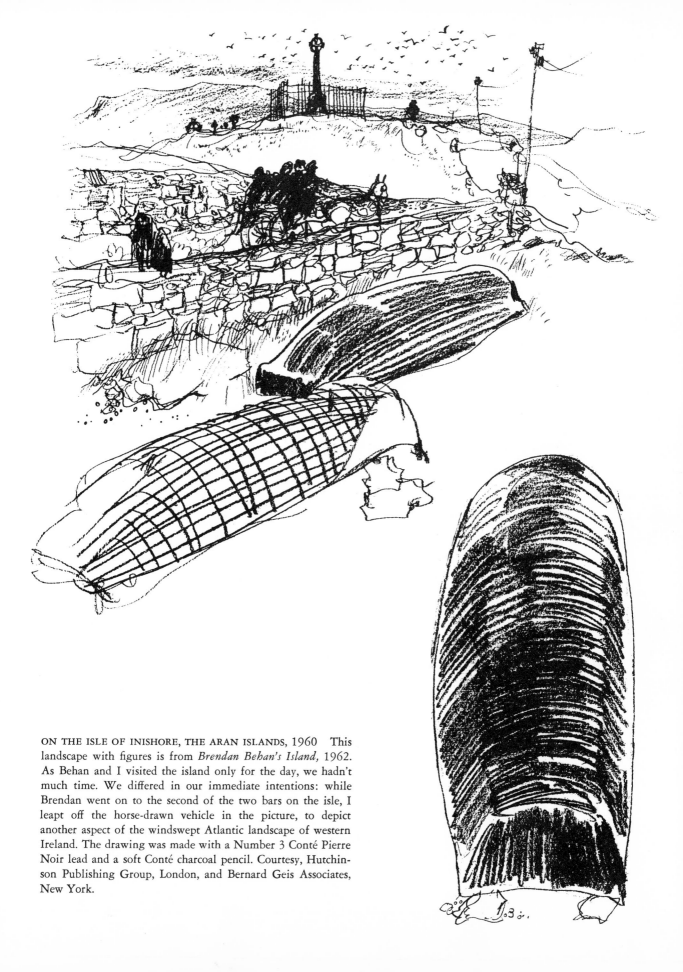

ON THE ISLE OF INISHORE, THE ARAN ISLANDS, 1960 This landscape with figures is from *Brendan Behan's Island,* 1962. As Behan and I visited the island only for the day, we hadn't much time. We differed in our immediate intentions: while Brendan went on to the second of the two bars on the isle, I leapt off the horse-drawn vehicle in the picture, to depict another aspect of the windswept Atlantic landscape of western Ireland. The drawing was made with a Number 3 Conté Pierre Noir lead and a soft Conté charcoal pencil. Courtesy, Hutchinson Publishing Group, London, and Bernard Geis Associates, New York.

WEEDING SPINACH ON A FARM NEAR PEKING, CHINA, 1954   I walked through the fields and watched the plants being weeded before I made a light, rapid drawing of the landscape background. I then worked on the moving line of farm workers, carefully composing the figures as I drew them in. The donkey and cart were added later. The drawing took about three quarters of an hour using a Hardtmuth medium charcoal lead. From *Looking at China,* 1955. Courtesy, Lawrence and Wishart, London.

Recomposing nature

I never really expect to find my subjects ready made. Effective drawing outdoors demands the imagination to reorganize and regroup scattered elements. For instance, I may be stopped by a landscape of undulating yellow corn fringed at the top by a strip of mountains. On reflection, however, I may feel that this looks a little monotonous. So I scan the terrain to see what other elements might be added: an engraved milestone, an artesian well, a tree or two, might make this into a more dramatic composition.

Again, the seashore does not appear at first glance to have the same variety as landscape. But if I make focal points of marine objects such as anchors, nets, or boats, then the eternal elements of waves, rock, and sand can be composed into intense and varied drawings.

Technique of direct drawing outdoors

When I start to make a series of drawings, I always imagine making the most extraordinary images. But I know that this will be difficult. Memories of past failures return to threaten my morale. So I seek, quite deliberately, to reduce the confusion caused by an inevitable conflict between what I would *like* to do and what I am *able* to do.

Before I begin my finished drawings, therefore, I look over my notes and decide to start with one I feel fairly certain will work out successfully. Bringing off the first drawing usually gives me sufficient lift to go on with the others, even though the second and third may fall below expectations. This psychological device helps build up my self-confidence, not only to begin, but also to complete what I have started out to achieve.

If I work with rough notes beside me, I use them only as a general guide to help me organize a direct drawing. But frequently, as I have already mentioned, I draw right away without any preliminaries. I usually begin to draw in a restrained or buoyant mood, which develops into complete enthusiasm as the drawing progresses. But like most artists, I have good days *and* bad days when my mood is likely to give way to complete despair!

I make myself comfortable with all my pencils, fixatives, and erasers nearby. With my hand above the paper—not resting on the surface—I draw swiftly and cleanly, working from top to bottom. First, I use a hard or medium pencil, then a softer degree; but sometimes it may be the other way round. After I have about a third of the drawing in, I usually apply a first spray of fixative, to prevent smudging. Resting my hand on a sheet of tracing paper, I then evolve the detail, working over the drawing as a whole, or section by section. Textural areas are freely exploited and developed. I may enlarge, distort, or reduce elements and objects which look more effective when they are drawn that way. These may not always come off, so I rough them out on the small sheet of tracing paper if I have any doubts.

It frequently happens that half way through I lose interest, not so much out of a sense of failure to interpret what initially attracted me, but out of a feeling that my drawing is somehow static and lacks tension. Often this may be nothing more than a lack of incidental movement at a single point of the composition. A flock of sheep, some passing or working figures, or a moving machine, effectively traversing the foreground, could provide the necessary compositional tension. I rough them out on the handpaper before drawing in. I look out for such details right from the beginning. Even if I do not need them, I make a note in a pocket sketchbook; afterwards, when I am miles away, I may want to use them after all.

My whole attitude towards drawing is so flexible and improvised that I seldom know exactly when I should stop. Usually, a drawing is finished when I feel I have largely—or partly—succeeded in abstracting or interpreting what I originally saw. I do not feel obligated to cover every inch of the paper. Once the drawing is finished, it may seem like a personal triumph or an anticlimax, or both. Having got to know every inch of the drawing, I do not look at it again for three or four days, perhaps longer. Then I am able to do so dispassionately: if it does not come off, I just tear the drawing up.

FARMSTEAD NEAR VIRGINIA, COUNTY MEATH, IRELAND, 1964 This landscape was one of a series of drawings made on location for a graphic mural in the Shelbourne Hotel, Dublin. Winter landscapes are sometimes difficult to find and then to draw. In the weeks before spring, however, the weather is mild enough to draw outdoors without being frozen to death. The trees are spidery black against lowering skies, forcing contrasts that are good to draw in pencil media. I built up this composition by bringing the farmhouse and hay-ricks from each side and holding a great black tree in the center; it was an arrangement in black, white, and gray, expressive of the landscape of County Meath. The drawing was made on Saunders paper with 6B and 7B Venus graphite pencils. Courtesy, The Shelbourne Hotel, Dublin.

LANDSCAPE NEAR ALFABIA, MALLORCA, 1963 This landscape brings together a variety of elements that were not really "in the picture." I had drawn the mountains with its layers of almond groves at the top, and decided to repeat this strip movement by textural emphasis on the stone wall, grass, and highway. This was relieved by a group of contorted olive trees which I moved in from outside the picture. It took about an hour and a half to make this drawing with 3B and 5B Faber graphite pencils. From a forthcoming book on Mallorca with Robert Graves. Courtesy, Cassell and Company, London, and Doubleday and Company, New York.

COASTAL LANDSCAPE, MALLORCA, 1963   The starkly primeval elements of sun and sea combine to make intense seascapes in tropical and near-tropical countries. This drawing of the northern coast of Mallorca, near Estallenchs, was made with a 6B Venus graphite pencil on white Saunders paper. To express the dying heat of the setting sun, I exaggerated its size and rays. From a forthcoming book on Mallorca with Robert Graves. Courtesy, Cassell and Company, London, and Doubleday and Company, New York.

THE MEETING OF THE YANGTSE AND THE KIALANG AT CHUNGKING,
CHINA, 1954 The old quarter of Chungking straddles a peninsula,
formed by the two merging rivers, and looks as ancient as mankind itself.
At its foot are a myriad bamboo-stilted dwellings. The masts of countless
river craft formed a yellow thicket against the blackness of wood-smoke
haze. But this was all so far away that any linear definition was hard to
make. So I drew alternately with washes of diluted Chinese stick ink, soft
and hard Hardtmuth charcoal leads. In the warm atmosphere, the ink
washes dried quickly, enabling me to draw crisply on them with a charcoal
lead. From *Looking at China,* 1955. Courtesy, Lawrence and Wishart,
London.

54

FISH EAGLES, CHINA, 1954 I saw this scene of fishermen using cormorants (Chinese call them eagles) at sunset. The flat, high horizon of the great Yangtse River, near Hankow, suggested a composition of partially silhouetted shapes, moving and working like shadows against the wide expanse of water. I had only a half-hour to work against the failing light, for later that night I would be on a train to Canton. I used a soft Hardtmuth lead to draw the men, birds, and boats. Once they had passed, I drew in the background of hills and nets with a Conté Pierre Noir Number 3. From *Looking at China*, 1955. Courtesy, Lawrence and Wishart, London.

YANGTSE BOATMEN, CHINA, 1954   This fast-moving subject again called for rapid drawing with a single medium grade lead. This was a difficult drawing, as I had to fall back over a succession of rocks to keep the same distance between myself and the sailors as they hauled their craft. From *Looking at China*, 1955. Courtesy, Lawrence and Wishart, London.

RICE FIELDS IN SZECHUAN, CHINA, 1954 The landscape of Szechuan has been likened to a vast sculpture. Countless generations have shaped the hills, widening and building up the terraces that hold the water to nourish the precious rice. In the yellow-emerald fields, the peasants still work as their forefathers did, wading through the soft, fine mud, ploughing with a wooden frame pulled by a wallowing water buffalo. I made the drawing in drizzling rain, inside and outside a car, in the early evening. I used a soft Hardtmuth charcoal lead for the landscape itself, and a Number 3 Conté Pierre Noir charcoal lead for the figures. From *Looking at China,* 1955. Courtesy, Lawrence and Wishart, London.

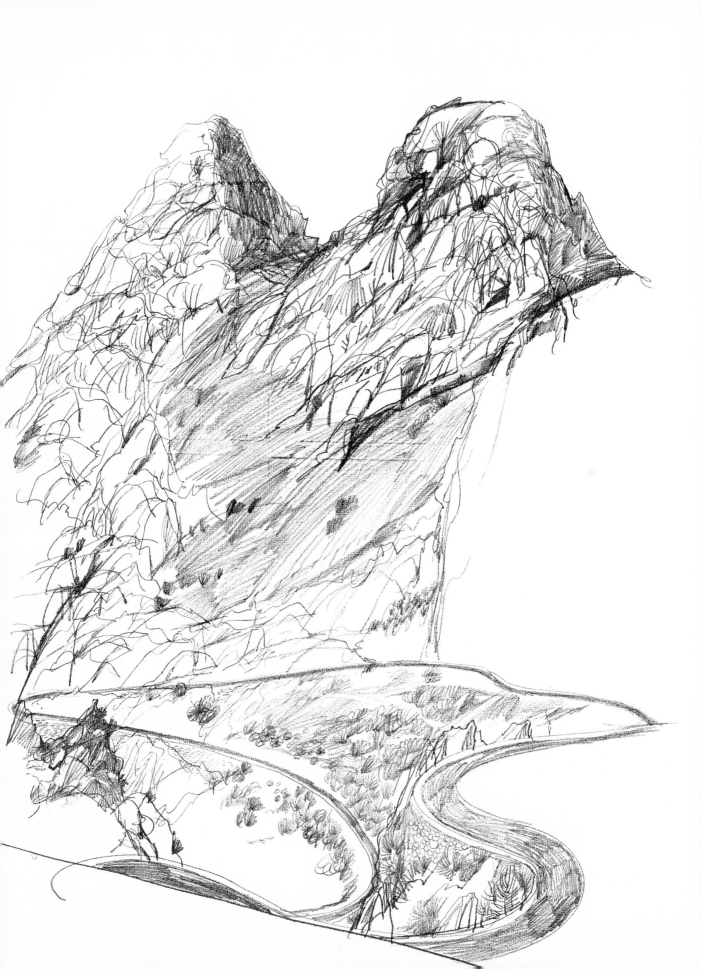

HIGH SIERRAS OF NORTHERN MALLORCA, 1963
Drawn in the summer, this is an example of landscape without figures. To express the rolling gran-
deur of this part of Spain, I emphasized the thrust
and sweep of rock and road. Two grades of Venus
graphite pencil, 3B and 6B, were used on white
Saunders laid paper. From a forthcoming book on
Mallorca with Robert Graves. Courtesy, Cassell
and Company, London, and Doubleday and Company, New York.

CONNEMARA SEASCAPE NEAR BEALANDANGAN
Drawn in 1960 with two grades of charcoal lead.
The heavier accents were drawn with a soft
Hardtmuth lead, the lighter with a Conté Pierre
Noir Number 3. The figure of the fisherman was
noted in a pocket sketchbook and afterwards
drawn in pen line. From *Brendan Behan's Island,*
1962. Courtesy, Hutchinson Publishing Group,
London, and Bernard Geis Associates, New York.

CONNEMARA FARMSTEAD, 1960 This scene shows how atmosphere can enhance a landscape. In bright sunshine, I had not found the scene so interesting. But an approaching storm introduced drama. Made at great speed on rose-tinted Abbey pastel paper, with soft and medium Hardtmuth charcoal leads. From *Brendan Behan's Island*, 1962. Courtesy, Hutchinson Publishing Group, London, and Bernard Geis Associates, New York.

STUDY OF AN ANCESTRAL HOME, SLIGO, IRELAND Landscapes which provide a setting for gracious old houses abound everywhere, but some of the more romantic are found in Ireland. The rational severity of the eighteenth century architecture is enhanced by the uninhibited ivy and overgrown grasses. Drawn entirely with a Conté Pierre Noir Number 3 charcoal lead. I used a graphite pencil as a ruler for the main lines of the house. From *Brendan Behan's Island,* 1962. Courtesy, Hutchinson Publishing Group, London, and Bernard Geis Associates, New York.

ARAN: THE HARBOR OF KILRONAN, 1960 This seascape with marine objects and buildings was drawn in about an hour with a Conté Pierre Noir Number 3. From *Brendan Behan's Island,* 1962. Courtesy, Hutchinson Publishing Group, London, and Bernard Geis Associates, New York.

5 DRAWING ARCHITECTURE AND THE CITY

FEW EXPERIENCES are comparable to that of seeing a new city for the first time, a city you have previously known only through movies, television, or books: then to live in it with butterflies in your stomach each day; to be part of its life; to watch its moods and tensions; to discover its idiosyncrasies.

You may love or hate cities, but they are complex entities of buildings and people, offering an immense range of material. The life that ebbs and flows in railroad stations, markets, and subways is no less fascinating than the life which moves against the background of fine architecture. And the very spontaneity of the pencil makes it the ideal medium to record and interpret it all.

Discovering a city's character

Because I was raised in a city, I draw city life with intense emotional involvement. Different elements of this emotional involvement move me to draw. Probably the most decisive emotion is nostalgia: nostalgia for the things and places I loved as a boy, like the old junk shops, flea markets, corner sweetshops, decrepit movie houses, Victorian cemeteries, and amusement arcades. These were once an intimate part of my everyday world. I gravitate towards them in every city I visit.

Style and elegance move me almost as much as nostalgia. In architecture, I like the dramatic impetuosity of baroque and the cool formality of eighteenth century classicism no less than the way-out fantasies of the nineteenth century.

The essential character of a city—its contrast and variety—is what really appeals to me. I am constantly stimulated by seeing vintage hotels and suspension bridges, old plants and ferries, cheek by jowl with thrusting skyscrapers and flashing motorways.

Cities are as personal as people. Capitals of past and present—like Edinburgh, Dublin, London, Leningrad, Paris, Prague, Rome, Warsaw, Vienna—possess superb architecture, which gives grace and elegance to all movement in their streets. Their individual characteristics are too numerous to list, but in each city, the habits and memorabilia of the past are found around you: the vast squares, the silent palaces, the shaded avenues, and the rivers with their ornate bridges.

Then there are the great financial and commercial centers, which have their own kind of atmosphere. London, Moscow, New York, Shanghai, and Johannesburg are shaped more by their present than by their past; in contrast with older buildings, steel and glass express the urgency and the increased tempo of modern life.

Then there are the older industrial cities like Barcelona, Belfast, Manchester, Liverpool, Pittsburgh, and St. Louis. These are cities whose aesthetic potentialities frequently escape the casual observer.

There is *something* worth discovering and drawing in every city.

Planning your drawings

The cities I draw best are those I am visiting for the first time. I see them freshly because I have *not* known them for a lifetime. However, I *do* like to spend as much time as possible drawing them.

DRESDEN, GERMANY, 1960 The essential nobility of the classical style remains eternal in this stark, burnt-out shell of a baroque church. Drawn against the afternoon sun with a soft Hardtmuth charcoal lead. Detail in the right foreground was drawn with Conté Pierre Noir leads 2 and 3.

65

Depending on the length of my stay (or "raid"), I start by taking notes in a pocket sketchbook, as usual. If I have at least a week, I can spend a leisurely day journeying around in a bus or taxi, or driving myself, making the same kind of visual notes I do when drawing landscapes. Although I am a raw mass of unresolved ideas and impulses until I complete the first drawing, these notes do enable me to think how I might carry out my plans. The notebook habit helps me to digest a build-up of conflicting ideas and to decide on just what is essential about a city.

What follows when I go ahead on the actual drawings, however, is another matter! It is often a combination of pure intuition and luck. Hardly anything comes out *quite* as I have foreseen it. Making a good drawing is like striking a match in the wind.

To draw well *anywhere* certainly means sensitive and spontaneous awareness of what passes before your eyes. I do not just mean how things may look on the surface. I mean their *significance*. A draftsman is an observer, but he should infuse what he sees with the imagination of a subconscious mind stuffed with a lifelong collection of experiences, loved *and* hated. The quality, size, and range of the collection have a real bearing on the originality and authority of a drawing. The city, therefore, makes different demands than does landscape or portrait drawing.

Drawing buildings

When you draw buildings—as when you draw landscapes—the time of day is important. The mood and atmosphere of a street, a square, or a historical edifice can change dramatically with the movement of the sun, or the time of the year.

Buildings of various styles are best drawn at a time of day appropriate to their character, and to the effect they have on you. I have drawn gothic and baroque cathedrals against a declining afternoon sun or a pale wintry light, because the partial silhouette effect enhanced what seemed to me their innate and absolute mystery. On the other hand, Victorian city halls or state capitols often have to be drawn in the morning light, because you must clearly see the extravagant detail of nineteenth century masonry.

Incidental ornament, signs, and lettering are a vital part of the iconography of the city. I fully exploit these to help convey a sense of period. I do not always draw them as I see them, but freely distort their size and shape. I place them in empty areas and spaces, or against colored, textured, or solid backgrounds.

Whatever the type of building, I first make certain that my drawing will fit on the sheet. This may seem an obvious point to mention, but when you are carried away by the sight of an unusual piece of architecture, you may not always realize what distance has to be put between you and the building. I have often omitted this calculation in a state of enthusiasm, regretting it later when there is only space for part of what I wanted to draw. By then, I may not feel like starting all over again, even if I had the time.

I sometimes get round this difficulty by continuing the drawing on another sheet. Later, the sheets can be joined with gummed tape. If you have to do this, avoid "bleeding" your drawing off the sheet. Break the composition at a point where some detail, strongly vertical or horizontal, will help to conceal the join. Frequently, to avoid such carpentry, I have simply used my incomplete building as a background for a composition of passing figures.

The influence of an audience

If I am traveling by bus or subway in a city, I naturally keep materials and equipment down to a minimum. I choose vantage points that enable me to work inconspicuously, although I do not mind an interested audience. Drawing in the city inevitably arouses people's curiosity. While the amount of public curiosity may vary from country to country, even from city to city, an audience *can* be disconcerting. I myself derive strength from the interest and comments made above my head.

There are very few people who have not wanted to draw at one time or another. The poignant memory of a frustrated artistic urge or ambition may return sharply at the sight of an artist working in a busy city street. The layman is often obliged to devote a great deal of his life to work he has

no real interest in doing. He will therefore stop and watch an artist because, for the layman, the artist is a symbol of freedom, a symbol of a life based on personal choice, not necessity. The layman watches with a deep sense of humility.

Artists, on the other hand, are usually lone wolves. Whether they care to admit it or not, they need an audience, however temporary, to sustain them over their long bouts of isolated activity.

When I was working in New York in 1962 and 1963, making drawings for *Brendan Behan's New York,* I looked forward to each day's audience. I would begin by taking the subway to some unknown section of the city. As soon as I started drawing, it would not be long before the first audience of the day would gather round. "Are you *really* an artist?" I was always happy to answer in the affirmative, although another viewer usually answered for me: "*What* d'ya think he is, *Santa Claus?*"

As my drawing progressed, the size of the audience increased, and so did the comments. I would be raised to the heights by a pretty teenager: "Could you teach me, Mister?" Then I would be dashed with: "Maybe he's some nut, wid that beard like Mitch." I was amused by that enigmatic, affluent character who strode past on Wall Street singing, "*Your* life is just a bowl of cherries." I was stimulated by a discussion with a young worker, who asked me to tell him just *what* did I find worth drawing in the exteriors of downtown bars at midnight. Whatever was said—and in New York something always *is* said—it meant that individual New Yorkers cared about the way I was looking at their extraordinary city.

SHANGHAI, CHINA, 1954   This city lies on the vast delta of the Yangtze Kiang. The mouth of the river is so wide that you cannot see the other side. So I decided to make my only drawing from the top of one of the highest buildings on the Bund, the former Cathay Hotel. The panorama was superb. Drawn in an hour and a half with a soft Hardtmuth charcoal lead. A Number 3 Conté Pierre Noir charcoal lead was used for the background and skyline. Drawn on Chinese bamboo paper. From *Looking at China,* 1955. Courtesy, Lawrence and Wishart, London.

There are times when audience interest can be less complimentary. One day in 1955, I was in Johannesburg, drawing outside an African beer hall which was packed to suffocation. There was an excited hum in the air. Children chased each other under the legs of men waiting for beer or waiting for haircuts from street barbers. The air was full of polyglot Johannesburg street talk, compounded of Zulu and Sotho, with bits of English and Afrikaans, mixed with American slang. The comments of the audience began to shift from the cleverness of the white artist to the significance of the scene I was drawing. The conversation suddenly became pointed and bitter: "Only *black* sheep are sheared in the street!" "*Black* man's hair gets trampled in the dust, but in the *white* man's barber shops, they sweep the hair up to fill pillows!"

But no audience, in my entire experience, is more actively interested in watching artists than are the Chinese. They would display extraordinary curiosity about my drawing routine. I thought this was because I was a foreigner. But then I noticed that Chinese artists were watched with just the same avidity. For the majority of Chinese, drawing is what TV, picture magazines, and movies are for western audiences. I would work surrounded by great clusters of people, including hawkers and peddlers and hordes of children. Wherever I went, there would be scenes of utter confusion. A street barber once started to cut my hair. Tenaciously interested fishermen followed me for miles while I was making drawings of the waterfront at Canton.

In Canton, making a drawing of a tea house proved more difficult than I could have believed possible. I chose a position inside a store opposite the tea house, because I thought I would be safe from the stifling curiosity of the mob. After ten short minutes, a row of smiling faces pressed noses against the window. My interpreter, Tu, appealed to them, but only succeeded in attracting more attention. Quite a large crowd now began to press into the store. Tu suggested going upstairs; for a time I continued working from a second floor window. But gradually the whole scene changed; hundreds of bewildered faces leaned out of the windows of the tea house and a dense crowd gathered below. I hurriedly adjourned for lunch.

SARATOGA, NEW YORK, 1963   In Saratoga, hundreds of off-beat, ornately ripe villas, hotels, casinos, and stores build up a pungent atmosphere of bygone pleasures and riotous days at the races. Unfortunately, I could stay only a day, so I decided to make a composite drawing. The two hotels in the foreground were drawn with a 5B Venus graphite pencil; watercolor was added later. I then moved out to a superb old villa I had seen earlier in the day. This I drew with a fine pen. The trees were added with a 5B graphite pencil. White Saunders paper.

71

Over lunch, with two Chinese artists, I exchanged anecdotes of the troubles of artists drawing abroad. There was great amusement when I told the story of Edward Lear, recorded in his journals. Drawing in Macedonia in 1851, Lear thought he had escaped all observation by taking refuge behind a friendly buttress. Suddenly out rushed a pack of bare-backed, jackal-like dogs, raising a tremendous racket. Although Lear had a pocketful of stones to keep them at bay, they forced him to take to his heels and chased him, "augmenting their detestable pack by fresh recruits at each street-corner."

After hearing this, the two artists went into an animated conclave. They came back with the proposal that I continue drawing the tea house from inside a covered truck. Almost asleep from a heavy lunch of baked carp and doves' eggs, perspiring heavily within the canvased interior of the truck, I peered through slats and finished my drawing in an hour. When the cheated audience recognized me riding in the truck, they gesticulated their contempt.

If you can take it, drawing in the city need never be lonely!

LONG STREET, GDANSK, POLAND   The old quarter of the famous Baltic port of Gdansk (or Danzig) was almost obliterated during World War II. The fifteenth century city hall was reduced to a shell. With few exceptions, so were the fine old houses of the Hanseatic merchants in Long Street. I made the drawing while the houses were being rebuilt, shortly before the restoration of the city hall was completed in the summer of 1953. The city hall and other background detail were drawn with a Number 3 Conté Pierre Noir charcoal lead; the scaffolding round the houses in the foreground with a soft Hardtmuth charcoal lead. Paper was Abbey Mill. From *Drawings of Poland,* 1954. Courtesy, Wydawnictwo Artystczno-Graficzne, Warsaw.

THE BOARDWALK, CONEY ISLAND, NEW YORK   On both my visits to New York, I used to take the long subway ride to Coney as an occasional break from drawing Manhattan. In 1962, it was already fall when I got there and the leaves whirled about. The ferris wheel and the fun machines were silhouetted and silent. Immigrant families argued on the boardwalk. It was in response to this mood that I made the drawing. Eagle Charco pencils were used—grades 3B and 5B—and brush-ink line was augmented with passages of Othello colored chalk for billboards and signs. A 5B Venus graphite pencil was used for the figures in the foreground.

NATHAN'S, CONEY ISLAND, NEW YORK, 1963 The second time I went to Coney, it was still summer. Coney was alive with people. Nathan's attracted me for refreshment and the fascination of its visual assault. I remember the insistent onlooker who kept reminding me that I still had another Nathan's sign to draw! Affectionately drawn with 5B and 6B Venus graphite pencils in a Rich Art 14 x 17 sketchbook of rough cartridge. From *Brendan Behan's New York*, 1964. Courtesy, Hutchinson Publishing Group, London, and Bernard Geis Associates, New York.

O'MEARA'S, 1959   This extraordinary specimen of Irish *art nouveau* fronts a quay on the River Liffey. Plebeian in character, the interior is dominated by a huge iron stove. The exterior is dominated by a series of remarkable plaster figures, a mixture of primitiveness and sophistication in their patriotic sentiment. Drawn with great effort (after a session with Brendan Behan) on Abbey Mill paper, probably using a Number 3 Conté Pierre Noir charcoal lead. From *Brendan Behan's Island,* 1962. Courtesy, Hutchinson Publishing Group, London, and Bernard Geis Associates, New York.

THE BLUE LION, 1962 A convivial place where moneylenders to the
poor, dockers and their "shawlies" assemble daily for a glass of "plain"
porter. Drawn from across the street in a 16 x 20 sketchbook of Daler
cartridge, with a 4B Venus graphite pencil and a Number 3 Conté Pierre
Noir charcoal lead.

77

NOTRE DAME

PAUL HOGARTH '57

STAALKADE, AMSTERDAM, 1958   As in London and New York, a motor-boat trip is the best way to see Amsterdam, with its maze of old canals. The old facades were drawn with a well sharpened Number 3 Conté lead; the foreground detail with soft Hardtmuth charcoal lead with touches of pen line in the features of the man and boy. Van Gelder paper. Courtesy, Charles Rosner, Esq., London.

NOTRE DAME, PARIS, 1957   One of a series commissioned for publication as greeting cards. I resorted to an open type of composition, which enabled me to emphasize the ship-like dignity of the great church. Drawn with a Number 3 Conté Pierre Noir charcoal lead on Abbey Mill Paper. Courtesy, Gordon Fraser, Ltd.

79

TWO DRAWINGS OF MALLORCA, 1963 The Mediterranean island of
Mallorca abounds in architectural riches. Richly ornamented gardens like
those at Raxa (*left*), reflect both Roman and Moorish influences. Adjacent
to Palma, the provincial capital, is Terreno, where *art nouveau* villas of
the turn of the century (*right*) still dominate the hillsides above the bay.
In both drawings, I exploited architectural background to convey a silent
atmosphere of bygone indolence. Both were done with Eagle Charco pencils—3B, 4B, 5B, and 6B—on white Saunders paper. From a forthcoming
book on Mallorca with Robert Graves. Drawings courtesy Cassell and
Company, London, and Doubleday and Company, New York.

THE WRITING ON THE WALLS, BELFAST, IRELAND, 1959   In this grim industrial city, streets can still be battlegrounds. Slogans stand out on the grim brick walls like theater sets of dramas for which the actors are in constant rehearsal. The buildings were drawn first with a Number 2 Conté Pierre Noir charcoal lead. These were drawn openly so that the figures added later could be drawn more emphatically with a slightly softer (Number 3) grade. From *Brendan Behan's Island,* 1962. Courtesy, Hutchinson Publishing Group, London, and Bernard Geis Associates, New York.

MONASTERY OF ZAGORSK, USSR, 1954   This great monastery, near Moscow, is part of a huge complex of chapels, theological seminaries, and burial grounds built over the centuries. Although I was overwhelmed by its dark sense of history, I made the drawing primarily to express something of my reaction to the exquisite delicacy of detail. A fairly hard grade of Conté charcoal lead was used, Number 0. Number 3 was used for the darker accents. Abbey Mill paper. Courtesy, Miss Haselden, Wrotham, Kent, England.

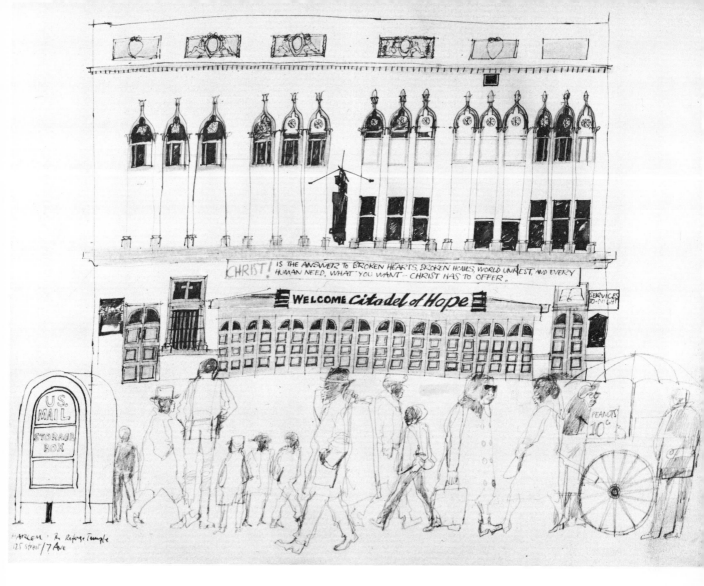

WELCOME *Citadel of Hope*

CHRIST! IS THE ANSWER TO BROKEN HEARTS, BROKEN HOMES, WORLD UNREST, AND EVERY HUMAN NEED, WHAT YOU WANT - CHRIST HAS TO OFFER.

U.S. MAIL STORAGE BOX

PEANUTS 10¢

SERVICES TO-NIGHT

HARLEM - The Refuge Temple
125 Street / 7 Ave

THE REFUGE TEMPLE, HARLEM, NEW YORK, 1962   The movement of passing figures against a popular architectural background: this is a kind of drawing in which much can be said about a city. Saturdays are good days to make these drawings, because every type of person can be observed passing by. The temple itself was drawn first in pen line. Color was later added with Othello crayons. Then the figures were drawn in with a 6B Venus graphite pencil. White Saunders paper. From *Brendan Behan's New York*, 1964. Courtesy, Hutchinson Publishing Group, London, and Bernard Geis Associates, New York.

VICTORIAN CEMETERY, CAMBRIDGE, ENGLAND, 1959   The wide variety of ornament in any kind of cemetery makes an excellent exercise for the artist who wishes to understand architectural detail. The cedar trees which dominate the composition were moved in to relieve the rather gray linear quality of the tombs. This is also the purpose of the figures in the center and immediate foreground. Drawn with a Number 3 Conté Pierre Noir charcoal lead on Van Gelder paper.

85

MANHATTAN FROM STATEN ISLAND

MANHATTAN FROM STATEN ISLAND, 1962 From almost any point on
the ferry ride to Staten Island, Manhattan looks massive and turbulent.
Yet from Staten Island itself, Manhattan takes on an intimate dignity
reminiscent of a Chinese fireside screen. It is a classic cityscape on a river.
Venus graphite pencils were used on white Daler cartridge. I began by
drawing the Manhattan skyline with 4B and 5B pencils, freely summariz-
ing the massed foreshortened skyscrapers. Then the foreground was drawn
with a 6B. Finally, I drew the river itself, with the various boats and
buoys, with a 6B. From *Brendan Behan's New York,* 1964. Courtesy,
Hutchinson Publishing Group, London, and Bernard Geis Associates,
New York.

THE HALFPENNY BRIDGE, DUBLIN, 1964 So called because in the old days a halfpenny was the toll charge for crossing the River Liffey at this point. Bridge crossings are good places to observe the movement of passers-by against buildings: you can catch movement *from* you and *toward* you, as well as across your line of vision. The drawing took a couple of hours to make, using 5B and 6B Venus graphite pencils on Strathmore charcoal paper. Courtesy, The Shelbourne Hotel, Dublin.

SCRAP DUMP, CAMBRIDGE, ENGLAND, 1960 Every town and city has dumps of unwanted machinery and miscellaneous junk. I discovered this one on the other side of the tracks in Cambridge. Drawn with soft and medium Hardtmuth charcoal leads on Van Gelder paper.

6 DRAWING PEOPLE

DRAWING PEOPLE, known or unknown, famous or infamous, may express your affinity with your sitter, but can also be an expression of dislike. Drawings in the first category are usually of friends and admired contemporaries. The second category is critical portraiture or caricature. Whatever my feelings about the sitter—positive or negative—the visual evidence of virtue and vice, strength and weakness, is what impels me to draw a human face.

Portraiture demands an awareness of people in all their frailty and variety. It is a social art which makes big demands on artist and sitter alike. You become involved with people often on the closest terms. To draw an effective portrait, you must exercise your *own* personality on the subject you portray.

First portraits

Although I knew what attracted me to portraiture, this knowledge did not help me much when I made my first portrait drawings. Under the sitter's watchful eye—unless the subject is an understanding friend—it is not easy to bring off an exact synthesis of character revelation (what the artist seeks) and sympathetic likeness (what the sitter hopes for). In my first portraits, I often fell under the influence of a sitter's personality and strove to create an exact likeness, which pleased everyone but myself.

Many of my early drawings were of peasants and workers encountered in cafés and bars, fields and factories, while I was traveling in Poland, Spain, and Greece between 1948 and 1952. Feeling humble beside these people who had suffered so much, I endeavored to please them by idealizing their faces, rather than seeing them as the intensely human beings they actually were. If I could have spoken their language, the tribute would have been more appropriate in words than in sentimentalized drawings.

Getting people to pose

The only way to understand people is to be in constant contact with them. I find that cafés, bars, and other public gathering places—both in cities and villages—are excellent spots in which to practice portrait drawing. So are waiting rooms in bus terminals, railroad stations, and airports. In Europe, South America, and Asia, you can find good portrait subjects in outdoor and indoor markets of all kinds.

In cafés and bars, the barriers come down a bit. As Brendan Behan said when I drew his portrait: "I don't care whether an artist is abstract or a realist, as long as he isn't illiterate or teetotal!" In this informal atmosphere, the artist will be accepted enough to blunt the oddness of a drawing being made, instead of a camera being clicked. Taking a 14 x 17 sketchbook, a zippered pouch containing pencils and leads, a knife or blade, and an eraser, I find a vantage point where I can see everything that goes on. If the place itself is interesting, I sometimes draw an interior with figures. If my initial drawing arouses interest, then I know my presence will be accepted; I can choose anyone I would like to draw from the people gathered around me. I make the request in an easy manner, like asking for a light or for change to make a telephone call. Being asked to pose is an unusual request that can only be made in a friendly, convivial atmosphere when people are interested in watching an artist at work.

THE THREE FATES AT SLATTERY'S, DUBLIN, 1959   In Dublin's quayside
taverns, the battered heroic-faced women known as "shawlies" assemble
like Amazons for their daily glass of Guinness stout. Among them I
found Mary Dignam and her two cronies. After accepting a round of
drinks, they sat for me readily enough. Then Mary rose, after I had been
working for a half-hour, and watched me make the finishing touches. I was
adding a line or two to her face when she placed a warm hand on my
wrist: "Spare the hand, Sir, I'm not yet in the grave!" Drawn with a natural charcoal stick on Abbey Mill pastel paper. From *Brendan Behan's
Island,* 1962. Courtesy, Hutchinson Publishing Group, London, and Bernard Geis Associates, New York.

I also use this approach when drawing in streets or markets. I interrupt what I may be doing when I notice a good face among the children or adults watching me. Children, especially, love to be asked to pose when they have sought you out and are watching every move you make. Much more difficult is the enigmatic person with a face you simply *must* draw; he refuses to have anything to do with you, yet watches with just as much interest as everyone else. Such people are usually shy about being the center of attraction, concerned about being made to look foolish. It is then that you really must use your wits to get the drawing.

The main problem of portrait drawing in the countryside, on the other hand, is largely that of winning the confidence of your sitter, who may have shown no interest at all. Although this usually takes longer than it would in a city, country people are no less fascinated by the dexterity and skill of the artist, and no less flattered by your interest. Country *and* city people may have to be assured that they are not being made fools of, and that *they* do not have to pay you for the privilege of being drawn. Country people relax more easily and nearly always are a delight to draw because they pose with little or no embarrassment. Moreover, they are used to sitting for long periods: for this reason, both countrymen and fishermen are good to begin with, if not to draw constantly.

Planning a portrait

I usually start a portrait by deciding how much I should draw of the person before me. This might be the head only, head and shoulders, a three-quarter figure, or a full figure. This will depend on the visual interest of the head, the general deportment of the sitter, and even the background in which he is placed.

If a head is striking, with great character interest, I will probably just draw the head, seeking to interpret the personality of the sitter. If the head is only moderately interesting, I might take in more of the figure, emphasizing more than facial characteristics—his hands, perhaps—and possibly introducing the background as an integral part of the portrait. Thus, the effect may owe as much to atmosphere as it does to the personality of the sitter. All these factors often exist in one subject and I will sometimes combine them in a single full-length drawing.

I now scribble a thumbnail outline sketch of a possible arrangement. This helps me in several ways. The thumbnail sketch pins me down to explore one approach of the many that will come to mind. I can now estimate roughly what distance I must put between myself and the sitter. All this saves a great deal of effort if I am working against time, and with a self-conscious sitter. For when you know what *you* want, your self-confidence is readily communicated to others and helps to create the necessary calm.

There can, however, be few rules after you have got used to drawing people. Your personal reaction will determine your whole approach, even to what size you will want to draw your subject. No artist sees the same individual as another artist does. At times, I have been bored right from the start; but on other occasions, when I was drawing unprepossessing sitters and had reconciled myself to making the best of it, I have made drawings I value most. For many artists, the unfamiliar face will be the one more easily portrayed. Overfamiliarity can take away the sharpest appetite.

What really makes for the creative practice of portrait drawing is your ability to appraise the potentialities of a situation from which a good portrait might emerge. And sometimes this will have nothing to do with drawing at all! So much depends on your personal reaction to a face, a gesture, a setting, or factors even less tangible.

Drawing portraits in industry

So far, the secret of persuading people to sit has largely been that of attracting their interest. This will not be so if you wish to draw industrial portraits, perhaps on assignment from a magazine or an advertising agency. Inside factories, nearly everyone is involved in complex processes of labor which may not allow them to stop or be diverted for more than a few minutes. Here, you will need assistance: someone who will break the ice by introducing you, explaining your intentions, and having the authority to stop work for a short time so that you can make a drawing. As most managements willingly collaborate with artists (and photographers), this is generally no problem, if you are working on an actual assignment or educational project.

Drawing people in industrial plants can be stimulating. Man's ingenuity is symbolized in complex work processes, accompanied by a wide variety of facial expression. This is particularly so in heavy industry—mining, for example—but less so in light industry, where facial expression generally reveals boredom with the monotonous, repetitive routine. Drawing industrial portraits can also be confusing if you do not stick to your purpose and are diverted by noise and stares. It is an exacting task, but one that can be overcome by practice.

Showing a calm I do not always feel, I begin by briefing my guide on what I hope to find and ask to be shown around before I start drawing. I make notes in a pocket sketchbook or in my head. I look for incidental details—eye glasses or shields, protective helmets, and special clothing—which might heighten the impact of a portrait in a dramatic or decorative manner. I also look for machines which I might introduce into the context of the portrait. By the time I return to my notes, I am more or less certain about what I want to draw.

In drawing portraits in industrial plants, I abandon my role as a detached observer and frequently pitch in like a movie director, handling

CONNEMARA PEASANTS, IRELAND, 1959 Never expect to draw country people on very first acquaintance. They usually like to know you a little beforehand. This drawing was made after I had stayed close to the farmhouse for about a week. The comparatively relaxed and diffident manner of country people is evident here, and this made it possible to draw more detachedly; country people rarely ask to see what you have drawn. Made on white Ingres paper with soft and medium Hardtmuth leads. From *Brendan Behan's Island*, 1962. Courtesy, Hutchinson Publishing Group, London, and Bernard Geis Associates, New York.

"BABY" SANDRA, NEW YORK, 1963   Weighing all of 280 pounds, "Baby" Sandra moves like a queen. Once a star, she still sings the hits of the thirties with swinging resonance at Sammy's Bowery Follies. As I drew her, a hand slowly edged toward a pack of cigarettes which lay on the table between us. Several seconds later, without moving or batting an eyelid, her great right arm slammed down on the impertinence. "You *must* be a greenhorn," she growled to a cringing bum. I made the drawing (at the heavy cost of four double whiskies) in a 14 x 17 sketchbook of Daler cartridge, with 4B and 6B Venus graphite pencils. From *Brendan Behan's New York,* 1964. Courtesy, Hutchinson Publishing Group, London, and Bernard Geis Associates, New York.

the sitter with all the persuasive charm that I can summon to make him feel at ease. No matter how much I add to the drawing afterwards, this initial posing or placing is vital for a successful portrait. I work faster than I normally do, as mounting self-consciousness is common to these occasions and threatens to "freeze" the sitter's features. If this appears sooner than expected, or bedevils the whole sitting from the start, I ask questions about the job or make light conversation. This is only possible, of course, if I can speak the sitter's language; but even if I do not, gestures or grimaces work almost as well to put the sitter at ease. I try not to make the session much longer than a half-hour. If a background is necessary, I add this after the sitter has returned to work.

Portrait drawing of this kind is almost a community experience. People generally feel happy with a portrayal of themselves or their work. If you can become accustomed to working in this way, you will find it a refreshing experience, whether you are an amateur or professional artist.

Drawing celebrities and personalities

Do not attempt portraits of the famous or the distinguished without plenty of experience drawing ordinary mortals. It is rather like speaking in public after being used to conversing quietly with friends.

Assuming that a face does not lack interest, there should be no more difficulties with a famous person than with strangers encountered in cafés, bars, markets, and industrial settings. Because he may feel awe or contempt, the artist may be unable to remain as calm and detached as he is with sitters he has never heard of. This may be particularly true if the portrait is not the artist's personal choice but an assignment.

I have never forgotten drawing several celebrities at a cultural gathering in Vienna several years ago. Among them was the Russian composer, Shostakovitch, whom I had kept an eye on for two days as he hurried around, whitefaced, clutching a sheaf of papers. Extremely withdrawn, with fine, bird-like features half concealed by thick eyeglasses, he vaguely agreed to sit for me. I had asked him for only fifteen minutes, but it was clearly an ordeal for him. He twisted in his seat, like a captured butterfly,

MALLORCAN FISHERMEN, 1963 Fishermen are seldom unfriendly to artists. Maybe this is because, like artists, they work in isolation. The strenuous labor of their working hours is relieved by periods of intense conviviality or relaxed conversation. These are the times to draw their portraits as I did here at La Calobra. I used a 5B Venus graphite pencil on white Saunders laid paper. From a forthcoming book on Mallorca with Robert Graves. Courtesy, Cassell and Company, London, and Doubleday and Company, New York.

and after just five minutes he leapt up to disappear into the crowded conference.

I shared his feelings so much that it was some time before I recovered my composure and was able to continue working. But the next celebrity on my list was the French painter, Léger, who was more than cooperative. Looking sympathetically over my shoulder at a bad drawing of himself, he said, "Not bad, not bad."

I find it easier to draw a celebrity if we know each other—at least casually—or if he knows of me. Of course, celebrities are more likely to unbend on further acquaintance and will accept the ordeal more easily. There *have* been times when further acquaintance has created tension, making things very difficult indeed. But usually, because sitters themselves relish the experience, according to their estimation of the artist's talent, they are interesting to draw.

I find writers to be the most congenial. They are nearest to artists and meet us halfway. Although Sartre was no less disconcerting than Shostakovitch—primarily because of his one piercing glass eye—he remained relaxed to the bitter end.

Political leaders are not so sympathetic, for they seldom let their hair down enough to permit a long look at their real personalities. Even politicians of principle assume pompous facial expressions which they imagine to be impressive. And those who are without principles are perhaps best caricatured.

As a portrait draftsman rather than a portrait painter, I am usually expected to make my drawing in the home of my distinguished sitter. This may rob me of a great deal of confidence (unless there is some sincere appreciation readily forthcoming). Although I never do know how I am going to get on with a sitter, I prefer to draw portraits of any kind in the sitter's habitat, despite the strain of unfamiliar surroundings. It is more essential that the *sitter* be at ease. I go through the formalities of arrangement and look forward to taking refuge behind my pencil at the earliest possible moment. When you have something on paper, conversation is easier.

Public personalities, on the other hand, are generally easier to draw, possibly because they are anxious to entertain. They may be extroverts or exhibitionists who know and mix with the celebrated. They may be celebrities themselves. Whether they are in show business or publishing, whether they are restaurant owners or barmen, they like to talk about the old days and are best drawn in the convivial atmosphere of a typical haunt like a favorite restaurant.

Doctors and surgeons are the worst sitters. I have found them unaccustomed to relaxing naturally. They are disturbingly aware of the passage of time. I suppose they are just not egotistical enough to indulge themselves. Also at the bottom of my list are a number of female dons, whose caustic irony so easily alienates the toughest male portraitist. We are but targets who venture too closely.

Looking at my drawings of various celebrities and personalities, I recall emotions of success and failure. Rarely have I felt that I had conveyed more than one aspect of their character. The only thing which comforted me was if someone who knew the sitter made an intelligent comment, suggesting that I had caught *something* after all. Failing the wholehearted approval of the portrayed, I may be buoyed by my own conviction that I have, nevertheless, made a lively and honest drawing.

DAME REBECCA WEST, 1961   I was commissioned by Penguin Books to make a series of portrait drawings of distinguished literary figures involved in the British Crown case against the publication of the unabridged version of D. H. Lawrence's celebrated novel, *Lady Chatterley's Lover*. The portraits were published as illustrations in the Penguin publication, *The Trial of Lady Chatterley's Lover*. Among the witnesses was Dame Rebecca West, and I made the portrait in her country home near Oxford. I was disconcerted because I kept remembering the superb portrait of Rebecca West as a young beauty of the twenties, drawn by Wyndham Lewis. I came face to face with this drawing on entering the house. Dame Rebecca's leonine head now had the beauty of maturity, but you draw maturity in a woman only under protest. And whether this is conveyed in a glance, in silence, or a whispered, "Stay your hand, Sir," one feels constricted. I continued drawing, but censure was tactfully withheld as the long afternoon drew to an end. The drawing was made with a Number 3 Conté Pierre Noir charcoal lead on white Van Gelder paper. Courtesy, Penguin Books.

Dame REBECCA WEST

Paul Hogarth '61

TEAK FORESTER, SOUTHERN RHO-
DESIA, 1956 This portrait was
drawn in the great teak forests which
lay just south of Bulawayo. He and
his fellow workers were waiting for
the wagons to be harnessed to a team
of oxen. Drawn in about forty minutes with a soft Hardtmuth charcoal
lead on smooth cartridge paper. From
Sons of Adam, 1958. Courtesy,
Thomas Nelson and Sons, New York.

BEMBA WOMAN AND CHILD, NORTHERN RHODESIA, 1956   African women are natural models. They will pose with great dignity for long periods and they disdain payment or reward of any kind. Not everyone gazes at white men with such good humor in this part of Africa. She was the wife of a copper miner and I drew her seated outside her house, talking to neighbors in the late afternoon sun. This was a good time to work: the women gossiped together; everyone was sufficiently relaxed not to feel an intrusion. On a smooth cartridge paper, I used a well-sharpened, soft Hardtmuth charcoal lead. A Number 3 Conté Pierre Noir lead was used for part of the drawing of the child. From *Sons of Adam,* 1958. Courtesy, Thomas Nelson and Sons, New York.

TINKER CHILDREN, CONNEMARA, IRELAND, 1959 Children are sometimes easy, occasionally difficult to draw. And it is always the most interesting ones that are the most difficult. The main thing is to capture their interest in what you are doing; then you can make all the drawings you want. You may have to go about this in a roundabout way. I made a landscape drawing to gain the interest of these tinker children, but I was only able to make drawings of them if I promised either to buy a horse for my wife, or present the eldest with a coveted picture book. Drawn with a Number 3 Conté Pierre Noir charcoal lead on Abbey Mill pastel paper. From *Brendan Behan's Island*, 1962. Courtesy, Hutchinson Publishing Group, London, and Bernard Geis Associates, New York.

MARKET WOMEN, DUBLIN, 1959 Drawing in markets in Ireland is no place for those who blush easily. In Dublin's Daisy Market, one of the few now left in Europe, old gramophone records of the twenties accompany the shrill exhortations of saleswomen, who sit like birds of prey among huge piles of old clothing, battered books, lithographs of Irish rebel leaders, and chipped medallions of the Virgin Mary. I sat down facing such a piled-up stall, waiting for the wisecracks. "Yer honor there, wud yer not lik to buy yer missus a gud pair of corsets now?" After repeated cries of "Take me photo, do!" I started drawing away with their cooperation, if not the cooperation of their rivals. I used a Number 3 Conté Pierre Noir charcoal lead on Abbey Mill pastel paper and made a quick getaway. From *Brendan Behan's Island,* 1962. Courtesy, Hutchinson Publishing Group, London, and Bernard Geis Associates, New York.

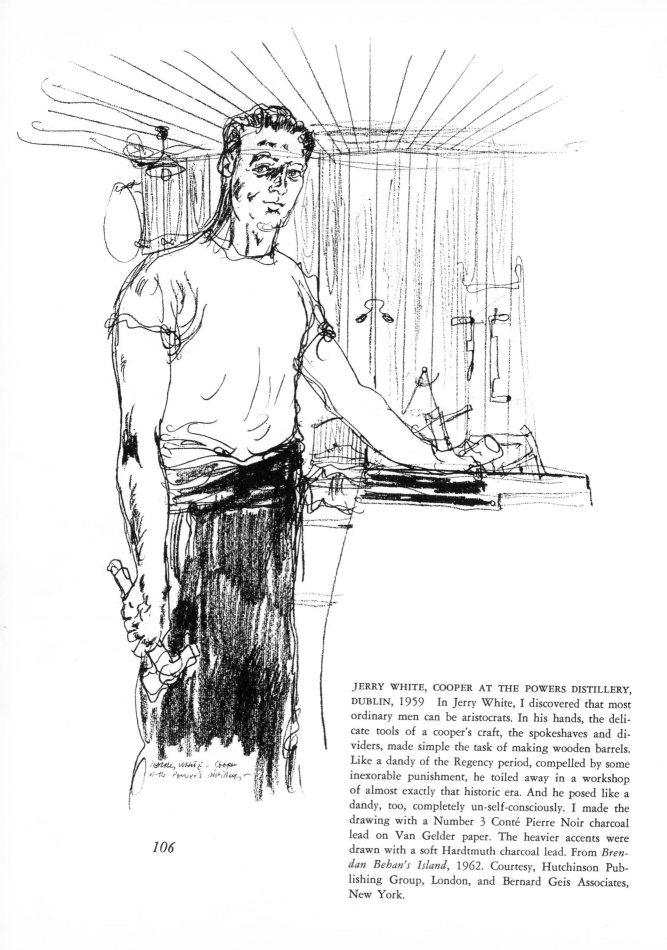

JERRY WHITE, COOPER AT THE POWERS DISTILLERY, DUBLIN, 1959 In Jerry White, I discovered that most ordinary men can be aristocrats. In his hands, the delicate tools of a cooper's craft, the spokeshaves and dividers, made simple the task of making wooden barrels. Like a dandy of the Regency period, compelled by some inexorable punishment, he toiled away in a workshop of almost exactly that historic era. And he posed like a dandy, too, completely un-self-consciously. I made the drawing with a Number 3 Conté Pierre Noir charcoal lead on Van Gelder paper. The heavier accents were drawn with a soft Hardtmuth charcoal lead. From *Brendan Behan's Island*, 1962. Courtesy, Hutchinson Publishing Group, London, and Bernard Geis Associates, New York.

106

MOSCOW TRUCK DRIVER, USSR, 1957   This drawing was made on one of those occasions when one suddenly sees a face that *must* be drawn. Somewhat forbidding and reserved when he realized a foreigner was noting down something about him, he started to edge away. When I showed him what I had done, he became interested and remained seated, thawing enough to allow me to continue drawing his portrait in public. Drawn mainly with a Number 3 Conté Pierre Noir lead—darker accents with a medium Hardtmuth charcoal lead—on Abbey Mill pastel paper.

GANG BOYS, NEW YORK, 1962   I was drawing a strip of Jewish and Puerto Rican stores on the Lower East Side, when members of "The Assassins" stopped by and watched. Sensing their intense interest, I started drawing them (*above*). "Wolf" and "Canary" arrived later and insisted on being in the act too (*right*). All the time, I was given the low-down on everyone who passed by, in the form of a non-stop, highly visual commentary which I wish I could have recorded on tape. I felt I had spent the morning with a group of highly articulate senior art students discussing the fate of abstract painting. Drawn with a 4B Venus graphite pencil on white Saunders paper. From *Brendan Behan's New York,* 1964. Courtesy, Hutchinson Publishing Group, London, and Bernard Geis Associates, New York.

OUTSIDE THE SYNAGOGUE, RIVINGTON STREET, NEW YORK, 1962 It was Yom Kippur, so I went down to the Lower East Side again. I took up a position outside the Rivington Street synagogue and drew various individuals as they came out. The boys, wearing the traditional prayer cap, seemed touchingly secure in their faith, in contrast to "The Assassins." I selected and drew the various figures as they passed, fitting them into a spontaneously conceived composition, starting from the foreground. The drawing was made in about an hour with 4B and 6B Venus graphite pencils in a 14 x 17 sketchbook of white Daler cartridge. From *Brendan Behan's New York*, 1964. Courtesy, Hutchinson Publishing Group, London, and Bernard Geis Associates, New York.

RIIS PARK, NEW YORK, 1963   Sometimes a street, a market, or a bar can be too friendly a place to work in. But a big crowded beach is impersonal. No one will bother you or ask questions. And not only do people come in every size, kind, and shape. They bathe, exercise, quarrel, and make love. This non-stop action makes a beach one of the best places to observe people and draw them. I built up the drawing from a continuous movement of people over a period of two hours, one September afternoon. Drawn with a 5B and 6B Venus graphite pencil on white Daler cartridge. From *Brendan Behan's New York*, 1964. Courtesy, Hutchinson Publishing Group, London, and Bernard Geis Associates, New York.

OLD REVOLUTIONARY, CHINA, 1954 This old veteran of the 1911 Revolution and the Canton Commune had worked in British Army freightships during World War I. He was a perfect model and remained absolutely motionless, yet alive to all that went on around him. While I worked, I thought about his crowded life, so graphically reflected in his dignified countenance. He looked like an emperor. Suddenly, he broke silence and turning to me, said, "Ow aw yew today?" This was the only English he remembered. He had saved it for the first Englishmen he'd met in many years. Such sitters are rare. They enjoy being drawn and are easy to draw because they are so naturally relaxed. Drawn with soft and medium Hardtmuth charcoal leads on bamboo paper. From *Looking at China*, 1955. Courtesy, Lawrence and Wishart, London.

ANSHAN STEELWORKER, CHINA, 1954 A skilled industrial worker pushes up protective glasses and you are surprised that he is Chinese. Who thinks of China having steelworkers? I would perhaps have lost my chosen subject on this occasion had it not been for a guide-interpreter, who made the introduction and explained my purpose. Amusement took the place of shyness, and I made the drawing in about three quarters of an hour with a soft Hardtmuth charcoal lead on bamboo paper. Collection, Bucharest Art Museum. From *Looking at China*, 1955. Courtesy, Lawrence and Wishart, London.

W. G. FALLON, DUBLIN, 1962 A source of endless recollection of the writer James Joyce. Fallon was a friend of Joyce in his Dublin school days. I drew him in McDaid's, a famous Dublin literary bar, in the company of W. R. Rodgers, the Irish poet. As the two reminisced about Joyce, Fallon revealed himself as an engaging, wistful personality of wry charm. I drew the portrait right off in under an hour, using a Number 3 Conté Pierre Noir in a Daler cartridge sketchbook. The flat side of the lead was used to get the stronger tone on the waistcoat.

WG FALLON - at school
with Joyce - in McDAID's
BAR, DUBLIN

BIDDY KELLY IN THE BLUE LION, DUBLIN, 1959 Biddy
Kelly, despite her unpopularity as a small-time moneylender
to the poor, aroused reluctant admiration for her raucous
street ballads. Her specialty, "Friends Today, Judases Tomor-
row," was intoned in a wild, strident voice with the edge of
an ancient file. It was a song with particular significance for
the clientele of the Blue Lion, which includes a sprinkling of
aged informers and other characters from the troubled Irish
twenties. Drawn on Abbey Mill pastel paper with a medium
Hardtmuth charcoal lead, plus a Number 3 Conté Pierre Noir
for finer definition of the bird-like eyes, tight mouth, and large
veined hands. From *Brendan Behan's Island*, 1962. Courtesy,
Hutchinson Publishing Group, London, and Bernard Geis
Associates, New York.

O'MEARA'S, DUBLIN, 1964 Taking out a sketch pad in a Dublin bar arouses relaxed interest, but little surprise, and you are likely to get a Guinness as a reward for what is generally felt to be a compliment to the house. Showing one of my favorite haunts, this drawing was made with a great deal of sadness. I had just learnt that the place was to be torn down by the end of the year. The bar itself is square and as high as a theater, with a tent-like ceiling, and vast, mirrored shelves. I started by having a drink, talked a little with the barman, then went to the back of the bar and started drawing. Never forget to show the drawing to the barman. Drawn with 5B and 6B Venus graphite pencils on Saunders paper. Courtesy, The Shelbourne Hotel, Dublin.

SLATTERY'S, CAPEL STREET, DUBLIN, 1964 The interior of Slattery's, a famous old Dublin market bar, makes a subject in itself, as well as a background for endless character drawing. Places like this should be drawn as they are visited, as they change so swiftly and are sometimes doomed to demolition. Drawn on Strathmore charcoal paper with 6B and 7B Venus graphite pencils. Courtesy, The Shelbourne Hotel, Dublin.

NOTTINGHAMSHIRE MINER, ENG-
LAND, 1959 This young miner was
drawn on assignment. The authori-
ties helped me find a good face and
persuaded its owner to sit for me. I
stood outside the pithead, watching
the men as they came up, and made
my choice. A guide asked the miner
to sit for me, telling him that the
drawing was for the National Coal
Board's collection. The miner stiffly
agreed and we went to a nearby bar
at my suggestion. Here he and I became less self-conscious and I made
the drawing in about forty minutes.
I used a soft Hardtmuth charcoal
lead, kept well-pointed, on a smooth
white Hollingworth cartridge paper.
Courtesy, National Coal Board of
Great Britain.

PORTRAIT OF A BUSINESS EXECUTIVE, LONDON, 1963 This portrait drawing began on the wrong foot. The sitter suggested that I should draw him in a certain manner. For a time, this prevented me from seeing how I actually *could* draw him, although everything turned out right in the end. Suggestions of this nature should be ignored. The artist should be quite frank, stressing the importance of a personal approach. This has to be *more* original than that proposed by your sitter! I asked the executive to show me his movements as he worked. It was his habit to sit on his desk, so I drew him thus with 3B and 6B Eagle Charco pencils on white Saunders paper. Courtesy, J. Walter Thompson, Ltd., London.

SIR STANLEY UNWIN, LONDON, 1961 This portrait head of the celebrated English publisher was drawn with a Number 3 Conté Pierre Noir
charcoal lead on a toned Van Gelder paper. I posed him looking out
through a window, so that the delicately chiseled features could be well
defined against a dark suit. Sir Stanley enjoyed being drawn; he gave himself completely to the occasion in his cluttered Edwardian office, close by
the British Museum. Courtesy, Penguin Books.

BRENDAN BEHAN BEFORE AND AFTER THE LOBSTER,
IRELAND, 1959   In the Connemara cottage where we
were staying, two huge lobsters had been delivered
alive. It was a stormy day outside. Flowers were placed
on a scrubbed whitewood table for the treat. Behan was
asked by his wife, Beatrice, to execute the crustaceans,
but he refused. When the deed was done by other
hands, he was up front, crushing the claws with the
repeated blows of his Italian shoes. "I like most things,"
he gasped, then pausing for air, "except wimmin with
rotten teeth." After the hilarity had subsided, I began
the drawing, using a Number 3 Conté Pierre Noir
charcoal lead. Restless and animated, Behan only relaxed after eating. I made two drawings: profile and
full face. "Time marches on," was his comment on ex-
amining the drawings, adding, "but I suppose I must
bloody well look like this." A thin wash of diluted
drawing ink was added afterwards. From *Brendan
Behan's Island*, 1962. Courtesy, Hutchinson Publishing
Group, London, and Bernard Geis Associates, New
York.

THE VETERANS, LONDON, 1954   The problem of drawing a group portrait can sometimes be solved by selecting a dominant personality, around
whom the others can be arranged. In this drawing of four aged cabinet-
makers, I decided to emphasize the round, florid face of the foreground
sitter, placing him against the tree-like gauntness of a standing figure. The
two less colorful characters were then added as balancing sidepieces. I used
a medium Hardtmuth charcoal lead throughout, plus a soft lead for darker
accents. Courtesy, National Union Furniture Trade Operatives of Great
Britain.

COPPER SMELTER, NORTHERN RHODESIA, 1956   The skilled African industrial workers of the Rhodesian copper belt are the descendants of the warrior tribes of the Matabele, undefeated by the British. And this tradition of independence still flourishes even in the context of the highly complex copper mining industry. It is also evident in their bearing as they work, tending the great crucibles of molten metal in the vast plant at Luanysha. Rapidly drawn with a soft Hardtmuth charcoal lead on smooth cartridge paper.

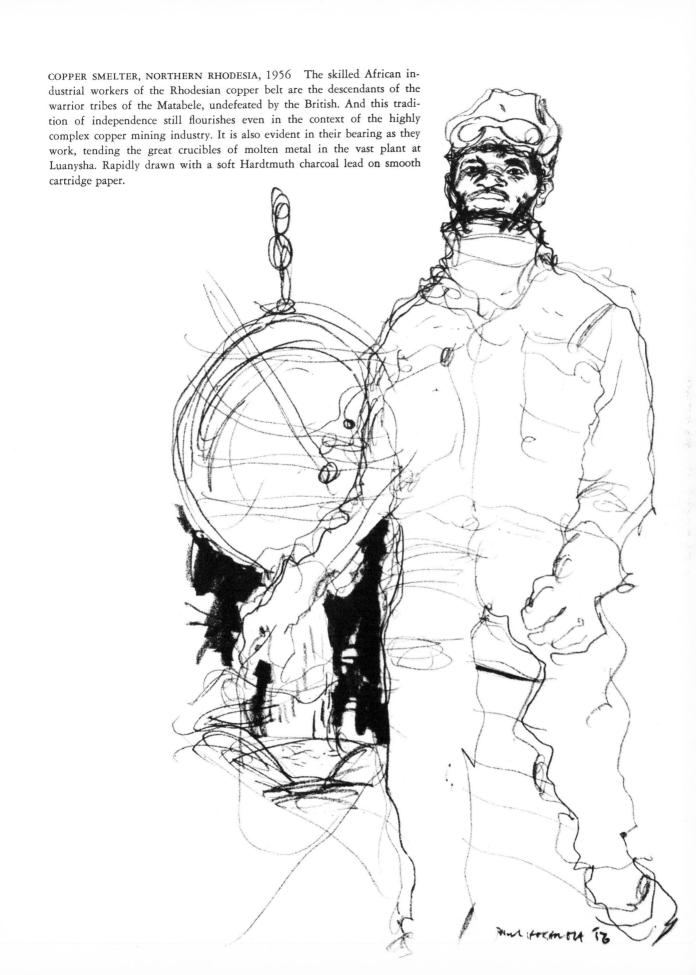

TRACTOR DRIVER AT A FULLER'S EARTH MINE, ENGLAND, 1960 One
of a series drawn for the indefatigable Charles Rosner, who accompanied
me and made the practical arrangements which enabled us to work at a
dozen different factories scattered about England, all to a strict timetable.
This drawing was made in fading daylight just before the day's work was
due to end. I had just finished a very large drawing of the entire mine and
would have willingly called it quits; but recognizing that the man was one
of those rare "naturals" who pose without self-consciousness for hours on
end, I made the drawing. Soft Hardtmuth charcoal lead and Number 3
Conté charcoal lead on Van Gelder paper. Courtesy, Laporte Industries
Limited, London, and Charles Rosner Associates, London.

TOMMY KANE, BIRDCATCHER, DUBLIN,
1959 Not far away from St. Patrick's
Cathedral is the Bride Street bird market.
Here thrushes can be canaries, brought in
by spry little men like Tommy, whose
pleasure it is to take part in a harmless
conspiracy to delude and delight the numerous small boys who frequent the market on
Sunday mornings. Made with a charcoal
stick on Abbey Mill pastel paper. From
Brendan Behan's Island, 1962. Courtesy
Hutchinson Publishing Group, London, and
Bernard Geis Associates, New York.

1 預防疫病. 講求衛生. 身體健康. 保証生產.
2 一致行動起來. 開展夏秋季愛國衛生運動.
3 滅蚊滅蠅. 防止大腦炎和痢疾傳染病

PEKING FISH MARKET, CHINA, 1954   This market drawing depicts a customer holding handscales, while an assistant selects prawns from a great stone jar. The banner, written in ink by an interpreter, exhorts all to observe the rules of hygiene: kill all flies; wash all produce; and don't touch the product. Drawn on Abbey Mill pastel paper with a medium Hardtmuth charcoal lead. From *Looking at China*, 1955. Courtesy, Lawrence and Wishart, London.

126

ALBERT LUTHULI, SOUTH AFRICA, 1956   I have not felt the urge to make many portrait drawings of politicians, but one exception was Albert Luthuli, the celebrated African leader and Nobel Prizewinner. He and his modest, self-effacing wife lived very simply. An atmosphere of domestic simplicity seemed to emphasize Luthuli's sternly aristocratic face, which could not conceal a warm and generous nature. I was moved to draw the man for his obvious integrity, but also for his bearing as a natural leader. The drawing was the second of two attempts and was made in about an hour with a medium Hardtmuth charcoal lead on pink Abbey Mill pastel paper. From *Sons of Adam*, 1958. Courtesy, Thomas Nelson and Sons, New York.

Tommy Kelly, barman at the 'Bee'
Falls Road, Belfast.
Paul Hogarth – '59

TOMMY KELLY, BARMAN AT THE BEE, BELFAST,
1959 Drawing on location is stimulating because it is so unpredictable. I was initially attracted by the ornate atmosphere of this bar and
started drawing the interior with a Number 3
Conté charcoal lead on a white Abbey Mill pastel
paper. Then Tommy Kelly appeared, with a face
that completely expressed the Edwardian-Irish
flavor of the place. But persuading him was not
easy. He was afraid of being teased and con-
sented only with the encouragement of his interested customers. What started out as an interior
with figures ended up as a setting for a portrait
of a warm and sensitive character, whose face
evoked the bitter-sweet songs of the Emerald Isle.
Collection, Sir Alec Guinness. From *Brendan
Behan's Island*, 1962. Courtesy, Hutchinson Publishing Group, London, and Bernard Geis Associates, New York.

7 PICTORIAL JOURNALISM

For almost a century, human artistry was the sole means of illustrating events. Painters, topographical draftsmen, and illustrators made the deadlines of weekly and daily periodicals before photography was fast and creative enough to record the momentary event.

"Our Artist-Correspondent" or "Our Special Artist," as they came to be called, were either adventurers with a flair for drawing, or professional artists with a flair for adventure. Between the two, every important event from 1842 to the first decade of the present century was reported in drawings.

Masters of pictorial journalism

As cities grew, daily illustrated newspapers, avant-garde reviews, and Sunday supplements gave artists even greater opportunities to report on the life of their time. Editors sent artists to report the human dramas enacted in lodging houses, night courts, and railroad stations.

The opening of the American West, strikes, bank failures, and night life were covered with boundless enthusiasm in a wide range of original pen and pencil techniques. This work, which might be defined as social reporting rather than news reporting, is of much greater interest than the purely journalistic drawings.

The work of the following artists, although a random selection, is well worth looking at in this respect: Paul Gavarni (Paris *l'Illustration* 1846–48); Paul Renouard (Paris *l'Illustration* and London *Graphic* 1880–90); A. S. Hartrick (London *Daily Graphic,* January, February, September 1892); Toulouse-Lautrec (*Paris Illustré* 1888, *Le Mirliton* 1887, *l'Escaramouche* 1893–94); Miklos Vadasz (*l'Assiete au Beurre* 1906–9); Jules Pascin (*Simplicissimus* 1905–14); John Sloan (*Masses* 1913–15); Kirchner, Kokoschka, Pechstein, and Nolde (*Der Sturm* 1911–17); and Dunoyer de Segonzac (*Le Crapouillot* 1916–1919).

A revival of pictorial journalism

Gradually, the camera eye—first in still photography, then in newsreels and television—assumed the over-all function of reporting news and social features. Photography has even appeared at times to replace the artist as a creative visual instrument. But artists continue to contribute various kinds of pictorial journalism to an increasing number of magazines and newspapers. A revival is certainly under way.

There are three main spheres of pictorial journalism. The first is drawing industry, or people at work. These drawings are usually made on assignment for such influential periodicals as *Fortune* and a whole host of company publications or prestige periodicals, sponsored by private or state organizations in both Europe and the United States.

The second sphere encompasses social events of various kinds, such as sports, trials, and conventions. These are reported in drawings or paintings published by *Esquire, Life,* and *Sports Illustrated* in the United States; and occasionally by the *Manchester Guardian,* the *Sunday Times,* and the *Observer* in England.

Burgeoning international travel is the third sphere of contemporary life reported by artists in a growing number of books and periodicals.

SORTING LEAVES ON A TOBACCO FARM, SOUTHERN RHODESIA, 1956
One of a series on tobacco farm life, drawn as illustrations for an article
by Doris Lessing and published in the English quarterly, *The Countryman.*
We visited the farm together and I was guided by the author in selecting
subjects. Such help is useful when drawings of specific situations are required. Drawn with a Number 3 Conté Pierre Noir charcoal lead on
Abbey Mill paper.

Holiday in the United States, and *GO!* in England are but two of many, plus a steadily increasing number of books which involve collaboration between artists and writers.

Drawing industry and people at work

Drawing the industrial scene or people at work is the most exacting sphere of reportorial drawing; but I have found it the most stimulating. Drawing industry is exciting because it does not invite reflection, so much as participation.

The encounter can begin outside the plant, in the gray calm of early morning. Tall chimney stacks belch smoke; crowds of workers are on their way to punch time clocks and start work. This is a dramatic scene at the really big plants.

Inside, the factory pulsates with sound and motion. And I am already there, looking at groups forming and unforming in the work cycle of people and machines. Assembly lines hum to the strident beat of pop-music. I try to restrain myself as an eager guide tells me all.

I cannot be literal even if this were desirable. I must extract what I feel may be significant in all the people, objects, and events that I am seeing for so brief a time.

Depending on the type of plant and the industry, my usual note-taking habit helps me to absorb something of what is going on. But this approach

CALCINERS, LAPORTE TITANIUM, STALLINBOROUGH, ENGLAND, 1960
This interior of a new paint factory in northeast England was one of a series drawn for a company which specializes in producing raw materials for industry. There was only one position I could draw from, so unusual was the layout of the plant. I decided to go for an impression of power, using an exaggerated perspective. The three small figures were included to further this and to give a sense of scale. Drawn on Hollingworth Kent Mill paper with Conté and Hardtmuth charcoal leads. I used a Number 3 Conté Pierre Noir lead for detail and a Hardtmuth medium lead for the heavier accents. From *Raw Materials of Progress*, 1960. Courtesy, Laporte Industries Limited, London, and Charles Rosner Associates, London.

only works if I am drawing in a self-contained unit, such as a factory. If I am down a mine, or flying along the thousand-mile-long construction site of a pipeline, chances are that I will have to work with no other preliminaries than a brief outline from an editor, filled in by a company public relations man.

In pictorial journalism, one can be swept away by a totally new experience with overwhelming speed. The expansion or operation of industry today is able to provide artists with an abundance of such experiences.

Working under pressure

Very early one morning in South Africa a few years ago, I found myself in miner's clothing, plunging down an acutely angled shaft at terrifying speed. A cigar-shaped car, reminiscent of Jules Verne, covered a descent of a mile and a half in three minutes flat, leaving behind a square of daylight the size of a postage stamp.

Wondering *why* I had to see everything before I could draw it, I clambered out into a passage little more than the size of a rabbit warren, and followed my guide down slopes that streamed with grayish water. Above my head lay the glinting strata of quartz and rock in which lay gold. Further ahead, the most extraordinary scenes of human labor were revealed in the ethereal light of carbide lamps. Hundreds of African miners toiled at the rock face. The air was stifling. At the end of a tortuous passage I had wormed along, I paused to look down a dizzy incline, where stalwart Swazi miners machine-drilled the gray rock face. The noise was deafening.

I began the first drawing sprawled against the watery slopes, with the light on my helmet feebly illuminating the sketchbook. Difficult as it was just to stop looking, the moment I chose to begin drawing was the flash point of my emotional reaction. I worked more rapidly than usual, and in a mood of unrestrained excitement, I hardly noticed what I was drawing with. At a moment of such intensity, *any* drawing tool might be the right one for the job.

What matters most to me in such a situation is immediate recognition of what should be extracted from the experience, then getting it down on paper while the whole thing has you in its grip. Not everyone finds it possible to work this way. It is an acquired method. If you find this impossible, work from memory or rough sketches. I would be the last one to blame you.

Planning industrial drawings

My usual method is to have a good look round, then return (without a guide) to that which interests me. After scribbling a rough composition note, I start drawing right away on loose sheets of paper or in a sketchbook. I ignore any noise or commotion, and concentrate on an aspect of a production process that involves one or several workers. I find such drawings interesting to do; usually, the typical character of a given industry can be well expressed. The movement may be rapid, so I wait for a repetition of movement to get it right.

In some plants, the machines appear to dominate the scene. This is especially so in the chemical industry. So I fully exploit the fantasy of their intricate forms which dominate, as they do, the few human forms who tend them.

Another kind of industrial drawing is concerned with the construction of pipelines, dams, highways, and bridges. This type of drawing involves many of the problems found in drawing architecture, except that the figures might be more prominent or active.

This is the kind of drawing which started me off on my travels in the early 1950's to record the reconstruction of war-ravaged Europe. The art historian, Francis Klingender, had told me about the draftsmen of the English industrial revolution, and I had marveled at his collection of lithographs made after the drawings of the construction of early railroads and suspension bridges.

Since that time, I have drawn industrial themes in America and Africa, as well as Europe and Asia. As a result, I cannot help feeling a grudging admiration for man's ceaseless ingenuity. An artist has to feel this very much even to enter a factory, let alone draw one. For in so many ways, a factory produces mixed feelings: a love for the more personalized life of *pre-industrial* societies, mixed with admiration for man's constructive genius, which inevitably destroys the charm of the pre-industrial world.

The artist abroad

Because so much of my book has been concerned with the various aspects of drawing on location, it is therefore unnecessary to add anything further about travel drawing. I *should* emphasize that for me it is the most congenial sphere of work; travel drawing enables me to practice every kind of drawing, in a variety of situations, with an infinitely wider degree of penetration. This is especially possible when I can work with a writer with whom I have a viewpoint in common, such as the late Brendan Behan.

Drawing events

Drawing industry makes heavy demands on one's energy, but drawing events makes equal demands on one's patience and initiative. This means adapting oneself to new or different experiences. I frequently have to grit my teeth to go through with the most depressing or extraordinary situations; I must swallow my pride, forget any self-consciousness or hesitation in carrying out bold ideas. But afterwards, the satisfaction of seeing good drawings in print is worth any temporary embarrassment or hardship.

Every conceivable type of drawing will be required and one should be familiar with the problems discussed in previous chapters. On the other hand, because reportorial drawing on location calls for rapid reaction, it may not follow that an all-round draftsman will necessarily make a good artist-reporter. You will need to work at developing a talent for being around when things happen—or are about to happen—as well as developing a fluent capacity to draw them.

Learning to draw in public

I first got used to working this way by going to all kinds of events where action was expected: stormy political gatherings, a prominent trial, or a

WORKER AT LAPORTE ACIDS PLANT, ROTHERHAM, ENGLAND, 1960 This is an instance of the way incidental detail—eye shield, mask, and protective apron—can help make an industrial drawing dramatic and informative. Drawn with a Number 3 Conté charcoal lead on Van Gelder paper in about forty-five minutes. From *Laporte News.* Courtesy, Laporte Industries Limited, London, and Charles Rosner Associates, London.

motorcycle race. I always knew the kind of drawings I wanted to make, but I always failed to make them. My drawings conveyed nothing of the excitement of the experience. Maybe I was too close to the audience. But, more likely, it was simply that I lacked experience: I had not been around enough. I realized that reportorial drawing was a genre that called for both discipline and urbanity, as well as creative dexterity. Baudelaire quipped that the famous draftsman, Constantin Guys, "had performed a task that artists disdained and which was left for a man of the world to undertake." This is very true indeed.

Whatever the event I may be drawing—convention, trial, or sports event—I naturally carry a minimum of equipment. I do take more if I am traveling where materials may be difficult to obtain, but I keep them in my room or in a car.

Learning to draw in secret

When you draw events, they usually have to be drawn there and then, under conditions you would normally avoid if you had any choice. You have to be prepared for the unexpected—like being confronted with a rule that forbids you to make drawings in public at all!

I found myself faced with this problem when asked to draw some characteristic scenes of the legal battles at the Old Bailey during the case against the publication of *Lady Chatterley's Lover*. London's Old Bailey— once the happy hunting ground of so many Victorian draftsmen like Keene, Hartrick, and Renouard—is a great place to observe the English legal profession at work. In a restrictive ruling which should really apply only to news photographers, artists have been excluded. Police are posted at strategic points everywhere.

My friend Ronald Searle, who has an excellent memory, once overcame the problem by retiring to the lavatory every half-hour or so, making his drawings behind the security of a locked door. I found it difficult to work in this way, so I tried (with varying degrees of success) drawing in my pockets in a 3½″ x 3″ Winsor & Newton series 34 sketchbook, afterwards using the sketches as a basis for redrawing.

Then there are the times when you've found a much sought subject in a particular kind of night spot or side show, but you are unable to draw because the owner objects. He warns you to stop or he will throw you out.

Sometimes you can avoid this embarrassing situation by asking permission first of all, making it absolutely clear that you are not a newspaperman or an investigator of any kind, but that you are making drawings for purely artistic reasons. (This is one of the times when a beard carries weight.) Even so, permission may not be forthcoming unless you are willing to spend a great deal of money. Somehow, artists are linked with photographers as undesirables whose activities may result in unfavorable publicity.

If such places are in your own home town and you are known, there will be little objection. Even if you are visiting, dropping by regularly makes everyone feel easier about your purpose. But if you are not a local boy and you are not making an extended visit, but you still want to get some good material, there is only one course left: you must make a drawing as unobtrusively as possible in a small pocket sketchbook or on small sheets of paper tucked into a book, then make a quick, unnoticed get-away.

Constructing a picture story

There will also be occasions when the range of subject matter is so wide that it is difficult to decide exactly where to begin. Under these circumstances, I keep firmly in my mind that I am going to tell a *story* as graphically as I can. In this way, I erect a sort of narrative plan that holds the whole experience together: I can add to this plan whenever I have a new idea. Somewhere along the line, there will be the opportunity to pull off *the* drawing I hope to make.

Like the time I had an assignment to draw the celebrated auto race at Le Mans in France. After making sure that my press credentials would enable me to move freely wherever I wished to draw, I abandoned myself to the holiday atmosphere of steadily mounting excitement. Following everyone into the vast track, I made my first drawing of the crowd moving in against a flamboyant decor of giant cut-out ads of auto parts.

My next move was to work out a rough schedule of *what* was going

to happen and *when,* over the next twenty-four hours of the race. I did not want to miss anything important. I also wanted to get an idea of when I *should* or *could* draw certain subjects. I also went round discovering the best vantage points. If I work with a writer on assignments of this type, much of this kind of information is freely exchanged between us. It takes much more of my time if I am working alone.

During the race I drew from one vantage point after another, trying to get a good general impression while the impact of the whole experience was fresh in my mind. I looked in on the pits from time to time, to make odd drawings of the frenzied activity of servicing and refueling.

Until now, I had been absorbed in reporting my reaction to the racing itself. But like other big international racing events, Le Mans is an unusual popular spectacle, with its own special kind of life. Throughout the day and night, the cars roar around. A gay summer fair changes into a Roman holiday, and then, at dusk, into a nocturnal fiesta. Rabelaisian scenes take place in crowded all-night bars and restaurants. Through the long, warm night, large groups play cards and chess while thousands of others sleep in huge stadiums. Vast quantities of fried potatoes, chocolate, and soft drinks are consumed by an audience that equals the population of a medium sized town.

My last drawings were portraits of exhausted drivers and an avalanche of newspapers and paper hats, blown across the path of car-carrying trucks on their way home. I was just as tired out!

DYKE BUILDERS, CHINA, 1954   Every now and then the Han and Yangtse Rivers burst their banks and threaten the three cities known as Wuhan. Several thousands of peasants were engaged in building a new dyke system with layers of impervious clay, using no other equipment than huge ramming stones. These stones were jerked up and down with ropes to the rhythm of a work chant. It was a scene reminiscent of the building of the pyramids; I tried to express something of this by taking just one section and filling it with action. Drawn with a soft Hardtmuth charcoal lead on bamboo paper. From *Looking at China*, 1955. Courtesy, Lawrence and Wishart, London.

The goals of pictorial journalism

No artist is expected to make a literal report of what he sees; otherwise, a photographer would have been given the assignment. Sometimes, editors do insist on the viewpoint of photography and the result is always disappointing; this always ties the artist down to an objective report. The *quality* of an artist's comment is what is appreciated by the discriminating editor or art director. A subjective, intensely personal interpretation gives an extra dimension to the printed page, giving it the kind of dramatic edge that the camera finds difficult to equal.

You may or may not find horse racing elegant. You may or may not find auto racing heroic. But you may well discover something offbeat and new to say, without feeling one way or the other. However you react, be as original as you want to be. You *have* to be, to beat the camera eye.

WATCHING 2600 MILES OF PIPELINE GROW   An assignment from *Fortune* to draw the construction of the immense Colonial oil pipeline, then underway from Texas to the Carolinas, found me in the southern United States in the fall of 1962. As always, the main problem was time. I had two weeks to see many different aspects of the project. The line was 2600 miles long and went through the back country of Texas, Louisiana, Mississippi, Georgia, Alabama, and South Carolina. Traveling by car or train would have taken months. We could only cut the time by flying.

There were four of us: two pilots, "B.G." and Bob; Ken Trotter, who was Colonial's public relations man; and myself. We used two planes. A big one for the long hauls from state to state, and a small one for the short rides. We would fly low over a section of the line and I would make my notes of what looked good to draw. Bob would then work out our position on his map. We would land at the nearest local airport, rent a car, and drive out to find the place.

I made my drawings in ditches and on top of huge machines. In little over ten days, I was thus able to make almost thirty drawings. I had never worked under these conditions before, recording construction done by rapidly moving modern machines. In China, although I traveled by plane a great deal, construction projects were characterized by their use of manpower rather than machines. But I found the challenge of working this way loosened up my drawing and helped me push out the dimensions of my reportorial drawing.

Fortune COVER   Surveyor Parrish at Spartanburg, South Carolina. The surveyors start their work on an advance section. Soon the machines will come. This drawing was an idea I had for symbolizing the planning that precedes construction. It was therefore very suitable for the magazine cover. Drawn with 4B and 6B Eagle Charco pencils, augmented with watercolor, on Saunders paper. Courtesy, *Fortune* Magazine © February, 1963, Time, Inc.

Thompson Ramo Wooldridge: Two Wings in Space

European Business after the Boom

FORTUNE

February 1963

THE PIPE IS BENT TO FIT THE CONTOUR OF THE DITCH This is done
exactly to specifications calculated by the engineers. Drawn near Cauderdale, Mississippi, with 4B and 6B Eagle Charco pencils. Saunders paper.
Courtesy, *Fortune* Magazine © February, 1963, Time, Inc.

A GIANT DITCHING MACHINE MOVES ACROSS A FIELD IN MISSISSIPPI It
traveled so fast that I had to move many times to keep up. Two perspec-
tives were combined to convey its effortless power. I worked from the
bottom of the ditch first, then drew the machine and field from ground
level. Drawn on Saunders paper with 4B and 6B Eagle Charco pencils.
Courtesy, *Fortune* Magazine © February, 1963, Time, Inc.

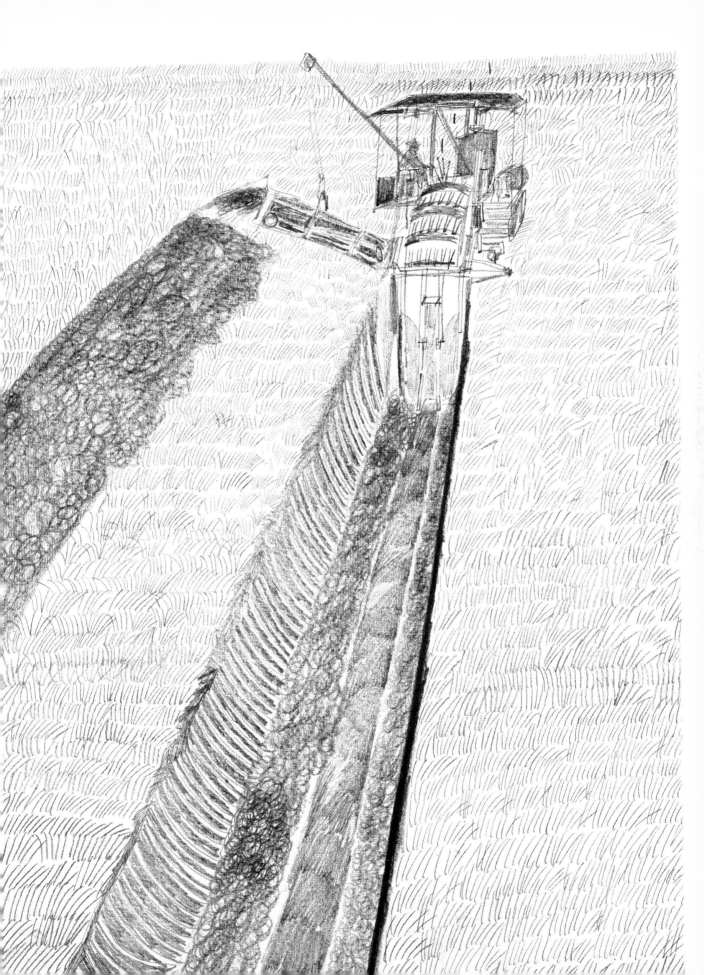

GREVILLE MANDER, LOUISIANA WELDER This portrait was drawn with
4B and 6B Eagle Charco pencils while the men took a short coffee break.
The American frontier still exists, but the skilled alertness of modern
technique has replaced nineteenth century muscle and brawn. This subject
was another symbol I discovered in order to characterize the pipeliners.
Saunders paper. Courtesy, *Fortune* Magazine © February, 1963, Time, Inc.

PIPE DEPOT The pipes are delivered from the steel plant to depots on
each "spread" of the line. Here they are assembled into required lengths
and X-ray tested. An X-ray unit is at work here near Cauderdale, Mississippi. Drawn with 4B and 6B Eagle Charco pencils on Saunders paper.
Courtesy, *Fortune* Magazine © February, 1963, Time, Inc.

146

X Ray Unit /welding PArt C

GULF

Coca Cola

Paul Hogarth.

PIPE WRAPPING   After the pipe sections have been welded, bent, cleaned, and primed, this machine cavalcade applies a coating of bitumen, and wraps the pipe with Fiberglass and asbestos felt. An inspector tests the pipe electronically for imperfections. This was a very lively one to draw, as it was so full of movement. There was only one way I could make it, however, and that was from a supply transport drawn by a huge tractor. I pulled out the whole scene in order to intensify the action and illustrate what was going on. I started from the top of my paper and worked right down, so as not to smudge the drawing. There was no time to spray it with fixative while I was working. 6B Eagle Charco pencil on Saunders Paper. Courtesy, *Fortune* Magazine © February, 1963, Time, Inc.

NEGRO CHILDREN WATCHING PIPE-STRINGING OPERATION IN MISSISSIPPI   After the ditching machines have finished, pipe is trucked in from the depots and strung alongside the ditch to await the welding teams. 4B Eagle Charco pencil. Saunders paper. Courtesy, *Fortune* Magazine © February, 1963, Time, Inc.

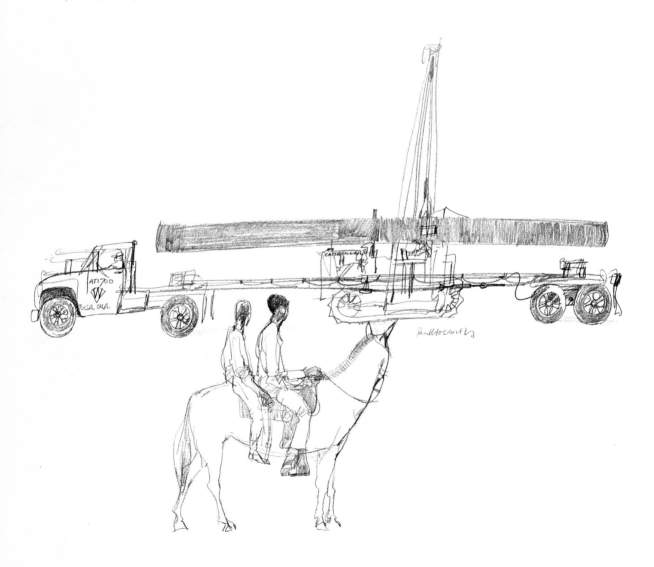

LE MANS, FRANCE, 1961 A general scene of one section of the track, showing the race in progress. The drawing was planned as a background "lead" drawing, leaving space on the right for the story title. Drawn with Othello colored crayons and a 6B Venus graphite pencil. Courtesy, *Sunday Times,* London.

THE EAST BARRACKS, WEST POINT Not an easy place to draw. I decided to do it by framing a fragment of military life behind a typical facade. Drawn with a 6B Venus graphite pencil with alternately applied washes of watercolor. Saunders paper.

150

THE BUILDING OF NOWA HUTA, POLAND, 1953   Nowa Huta means New
Foundry. It is near Krakow and is one of the biggest steel plants in
Europe. The drawing was made when the construction was half finished.
A Number 3 Conté Pierre Noir lead was used for the detailed delineation
of the background; a soft Hardtmuth charcoal lead for the girder structure
in the foreground. From *Drawings of Poland*, 1954. Courtesy, Wydawnictwo Artystczno-Graficzne, Warsaw.

152

AFTER THE DAY'S WORK, BULAWAYO, SOUTHERN RHODESIA, 1956 One evening, I was driving back from a day's landscape drawing and saw animated, jostling Africans spill out of a nearby plant. The next day, I arrived at the spot about an hour before. I drew the background with a soft Hardtmuth lead, sharpened three Conté charcoal pencils, and waited for the whistle to blow. The exodus lasted no more than fifteen minutes, so I had to work rapidly. Abbey Mill paper. From *Sons of Adam*, 1958. Courtesy, Thomas Nelson Company, New York.

BLAST FURNACE WORKERS (LEFT)   In the West, this kind of strength has almost vanished from an industry now almost entirely automated. Steelworkers of this type have much in common with miners and fishermen. They work with the same natural dignity. This was the quality I tried to get. Drawn with a soft Hardtmuth charcoal lead on Chinese bamboo paper. Collection, Bucharest Art Museum. From *Looking at China*, 1955. Courtesy, Lawrence and Wishart, London.

IN THE PLATE SHOP OF THE AUTOMATIC ROLLING MILL   Machinery and other background details were drawn while waiting for the trio to repeat their movements every few minutes or so. The slogan in Chinese was written in by my interpreter. Drawn with a soft Hardtmuth charcoal lead. Abbey Mill paper. From *Looking at China*, 1955. Courtesy, Lawrence and Wishart, London.

156

KUANG SO-YEN, LATHE OPERATOR, SHENYANG, CHINA, 1954 Made at the request of the London *News Chronicle*, to illustrate one of a series of articles by their special correspondent, James Cameron, this drawing stressed the fact that women in China get equal opportunities to be skilled industrial workers. Although the contrast between girl and machine had greater visual possibilities, the idea of a girl of nineteen working such a complicated machine, provided a good subject for a piece of straight-forward drawing. Girl drawn with a Number 3 Conté Pierre Noir lead; the machine with a soft Hardtmuth charcoal lead. Bamboo paper. From *Looking at China*, 1955. Courtesy, Lawrence and Wishart, London.

EDITED BY DONALD HOLDEN

DESIGNED BY BETTY BINNS

COMPOSED IN GARAMOND BOLD BY ATLANTIC LINOTYPE COMPANY, INC.

OFFSET BY AFFILIATED LITHOGRAPHERS, INC.

BOUND BY THE HADDON CRAFTSMEN, INC.

LAID STOCK SPECIALLY MANUFACTURED FOR THIS BOOK BY STRATHMORE PAPER CO.